Great Stories of World War II

An Annotated Bibliography of Eyewitness War-Related Books Written and Published Between 1940 and 1946

Arthur Coleman
Hildy Neel

Consulting Editor
Martin Gordon

The Scarecrow Press, Inc.
Lanham, Maryland • Toronto • Plymouth, UK
2007

SCARECROW PRESS, INC.

Published in the United States of America
by Scarecrow Press, Inc.
A wholly owned subsidiary of
The Rowman & Littlefield Publishing Group, Inc.
4501 Forbes Boulevard, Suite 200, Lanham, Maryland 20706
www.scarecrowpress.com

Estover Road
Plymouth PL6 7PY
United Kingdom

British Library Cataloguing in Publication Information Available

Library of Congress Cataloging-in-Publication Data
Coleman, Arthur, 1924–
  Great stories of World War II : an annotated bibliography of eyewitness war-
related books written and published between 1940 and 1946 / Arthur Coleman,
Hildy Neel ; consulting editor, Martin Gordon.
    p. cm.
  Includes bibliographical references.
  ISBN-13: 978-0-8108-5049-1 (alk. paper)
  ISBN-10: 0-8108-5049-4 (alk. paper)
  1. World War, 1939–1945–Personal narratives, American–Abstracts. I. Neel,
Hildy, 1967– II. Gordon, Martin. III. Title. IV. Title: Great stories of World
War Two. V. Title: Great stories of World War 2.
  D739.C55 2007
  016.94054'8173—dc22   2004005585

CONTENTS

ACKNOWLEDGMENTS

Special thanks to Richard Troisi and Dr. Darel Moss for their technical expertise in compiling this volume. We appreciate Dr. Edmund Miller for his help and continuous interest in this publication.

We are very grateful to Martin Gordon, consultant for Scarecrow Press, for his excellent and painstaking editing.

INTRODUCTION

World War II personal narratives began to appear within months of the Japanese attack at Pearl Harbor (Robert Trumbull's *The Raft*, first of this new genre, was published in early February 1942) and continued to roll off the presses well after atom bombs exploded over Hiroshima and Nagaski, ending hostilities in Asia. Marketed by publishers for those at home eager to obtain firsthand knowledge of the many faces of war, the number of these documentary reports appearing on the best-seller lists each wartime week testifies to their enormous popularity. The simplest explanation for the considerable appeal of these books was a natural desire of a worried public for more than stark and spare military dispatches printed in the daily press. Different from routine and succinct government communiqués that provided abstract reports of the many battles raging around the world, personal narratives offered remarkably detailed and generally uncensored disclosures of the grim and frightening conditions that fighting men endured far from home throughout nearly four dark and anxious years of war. Very much like their genre predecessors, which documented the hard times on ordinary citizens in a depressed nation during the 1930s, World War II narratives similarly managed to render the sense and substance of extraordinary and disturbing wartime tensions that beset the early 1940s, affecting the lives of countless millions home and abroad.

Realizing the potential of considerable public interest in biohistories of things distant and unknowable at a time of great national crisis, for both industry profit and as propaganda contribution to the war effort publishers allocated much of their heavily rationed resources of paper and ink to the production of these chronicles. Manuscripts were actively solicited from civilian reporters, servicemen and women, defense plant workers, government officials, homebound parents and loved ones, as well as members of many support groups in the all-consuming fight for national survival, and by hostility's end in late 1945 more than five hundred of these personal narratives had been published. Among the many reports of actual fighting on land, in the air, and at sea, from the islands in the Pacific and the deserts of Africa to the battlefields of Italy and France, were books of letters exchanged between soldiers and sweethearts, several written by Hollywood stars, military nurses, Red Cross workers, army and navy chaplains, merchant mariners, and army and navy correspondents and cameramen, becoming a genre accumulation of the total wartime experience reflected through American eyes. All in all, these documentaries satisfied the definition offered by William Stott in his seminal study, *Documentary Expression and Thirties America*, in that they helped to "increase our knowledge of public facts . . . sharpen it with feelings, put [us] in touch with the perennial human spirit [and] show it struggling . . . at a specific historical moment." Indeed, because of the writers' closeness to events, and the quickness with which the public received their reportage, civilian and soldier narratives alike managed to capture the full dimension of human feelings during the shocks and disorders of the times, with an avidness that most secondary histories are unable to match. Altogether then, these personal narratives published virtually during the heat of battle now represent a dust-gathering record of a special spirit in the American people in their scarcely remembered "rendezvous with destiny," stories minimally understood and uncertainly appreciated by passing generations of what their nation in the 1940s was like, and on a more meaningful level perhaps, how their fathers, mothers, and grandparents measured up when this country at mid-century was a different sort of place and countrymen a different breed.

Most of the entries recorded in this bibliography typically furnish brief critical and explanatory notes. In a few instances, however, expanded commentaries were deemed appropriate because of some special character of noteworthiness about certain texts. Finally, as an added informational apparatus, beneath most entries are dates and places where may be found selected reviews that were printed in the daily press at the very time these personal narratives were published. Because the reviews were mainly from six traditional review sources, we list here their names and the abbreviations used for them throughout the text.

BW	*Book Week*
NR	*New Republic*
NYT	*New York Times*
SRL	*Saturday Review of Literature*
WBR	*Weekly Book Review*
YR	*Yale Review*

Hildy Neel

BIBLIOGRAPHY

Abbott, Henry. *The Nazi "88" Made Believers*. Dayton, Ohio: Otterbein Press, 1944. 250p

   Story of a military chaplain who tirelessly cared for all the spiritual and physical needs of the men in the 13th Armory Regiment during the North African campaign. He tells of the hardships endured and courage displayed by the soldiers, and how he helped with the wounded and fallen, and comforted the weary and distressed. Sounding the note that "there are no atheists in foxholes," Chaplain Abbott explained "that the preparation for battle [by] a country of free men is . . . not only physical but spiritual as well."

Abercrombie, Laurence, and **Fletcher Pratt**. *My Life to the Destroyers*. New York: Holt, 1945. 157p

   Captain Abercrombie was skipper of the U.S. destroyer *Drayton* at the time of Pearl Harbor. His ship was one of the first to engage the Japanese in action at Midway and Cape Esperance. In addition to the fighting sequences, the narrative also describes what a destroyer is and does as part of the fleet and includes amusing, intimate accounts of life aboard a warship, from the eccentricities of officers and men, to problems involving pay, liberty, food, and hygiene. The gist of *My Life to the Destroyers* is that men not accustomed to war learn to fight and learn just how capable they are in the midst of battle.

   NYT 1/7/45, p7. 1000w

Adolph, Paul. *Surgery Speaks to China*. Philadelphia: China Inland Mission, 1945. 195p

   Experiences of a medical missionary to China in peace and in war.

Archard, Theresa. *G.I. Nightingale: The Story of an American Army Nurse*. New York: Norton, 1945. 187p

   Captain Archard, head army nurse in a surgical hospital unit, went ashore with other nurses on the first day American troops invaded North Africa and for more than a year cared for the wounded there and during the Sicilian campaign, dealing with the difficulties of weather, limited medical supplies, shortages of adequate food and clothing, compounded by the frustrations of army red tape. With the incredible resourcefulness of her corps of nurses, Archard set up field hospitals in the midst of raging battles to minister to the overwhelming casualties. The book is a testimony to the remarkable courage and endurance of a small group of skilled women in the face of constant danger and their rightful pride in the care and comfort they provided the wounded, saving many lives. This book is an eyewitness, day-by-day account of wartime battlefield nursing through the prism of an American woman who experienced it firsthand.

> *NYT* 7/1/45, p8. 550w
>
> *WBR* 6/6/45, p3. 850w

Archer, Laird. *Balkan Journal.* New York: Norton, 1944. 254p

A collection of remarks dealing with international affairs excerpted from Archer's experiences (beginning in 1934) as director of the Near East Foundation. Of particular interest are the descriptions of events of daily life of the Balkan people from the period of Axis appeasement to the grim reality of German invasion and the nightmare of Nazi occupation of their lands.

> *NYT* 4/9/44, p1. 1450w
>
> *SRL* 4/22/44, p11. 1050w

Associated Press News Annuals. 1945.

The story of a year written from the dispatches and pictures of Associated Press correspondents and photographers around the world. The book is a day-by-day chronology of every major event in the news of 1945, with the war and international politics given major expression throughout. As such, it contains valuable source material for World War II historians.

> *SRL* 6/22/46, p12. 1100w
>
> *WBR* 6/23/46, p14. 420w

Ayling, Keith. *Semper Fidelis: The U.S. Marines in Action.* Boston: Houghton Mifflin, 1943. 194p

Narrative describing the exploits of U.S. Marines in action on Guadalcanal, Wake Island, and Midway, much of the details based on the words of men who survived those heartbreaking battles. In addition to accounts of actions on the South Pacific islands, early chapters deal with stateside training and a brief history of the Corps itself.

> *BW* 11/14/45, p10. 1800w

———. *They Fly to Fight: The Story of Airborne Divisions.* New York: Appleton-Century, 1944. 191p

Descriptions of the paratroopers who jump from planes and the airborne troops flown by gliders into battle. Narrative is filled with information about qualifications, training, and the planes and supplies required for a successful operation. Most of the book is devoted to the careful selection of the right men to become "as cunning as a fox and tough as a lion . . . to do the fighting of ten" ordinary soldiers. In addition, Ayling alerts readers to the importance of airborne tactics now and in the future.

> *NYT* 6/11/44, p14. 400w

————. *Old Leatherface of the Flying Tigers: The Story of General Chennault.* Indianapolis, Ind.: Bobbs-Merrill, 1945. 274p

A straightforward factual biography about General Clair Chennault, a colorful soldier, and a motley group of airmen who made many successful missions—which caused so much discomfort to the Japanese in Burma and China—before they evolved into part of the regular air force of the American army. Ayling pictures Chennault as a rough-and-ready leader who inspired respect among his men but who alienated the establishment "brass."

NR 9/3/45, p293. 950w

NYT 8/12/45, p12. 500w

Babcock, A. E., and **Norma McKee**. *A Guy Who Knows.* Ramally, 1946. 123p

A collection of letters written by Staff Sergeant Miles S. Babcock, saved and published by his father and sister, in which the sergeant describes the fighting in Bouganville, Tarawa, Saipan, and Guadalcanal. His letters reveal a range of emotions displayed by weary, jungle-fevered Americans, hardened in the crucible of battles, sometimes grim, sometimes carefree under fire, always frightened but doing their best against the enemy.

Bailey, Gilbert. *Boot: A Marine in the Making.* New York: Macmillan, 1944. 131p

This is an account of the rigors of boot camp training which eventually turns a civilian into a fighting man ready for battle. The text is enhanced by the impact derived from many full-paged photographs.

BW 6/18/44, p6. 400w

WBR 5/28/44, p12. 200w

Baillie, Hugh. *Two Battlefronts.* New York: United Press, 1943. 123p

Dispatches written by the president of the United Press News Agency covering the air offensive over Germany and the Sicilian campaign during the summer of 1943. It offers a glimpse of the job that war correspondents do to provide a steady flow of information from all the battlefronts, as they are themselves exposed to enemy strafing and shellfire, subsisting on meager "grub," bivouacking on the muddy ground, or "wriggling up precipitous hillsides to observe the enemy" (preface).

Baker, George. *The Sad Sack.* New York: Simon & Schuster, 1944. 237p

————. *The New Sad Sack.* New York: Simon & Schuster, 1946. 167p

Taken together, these companion volumes dramatize in cartoon sketches and quasi-sadistic captions the experiences of an Everyman G.I. suffering the adversities typical of military life. Crushed by the deadly dull army routines, Baker's bewildered antihero caricature has valid semblance to many World War II soldiers.

SRL 10/14/44, p56. 550w

NYT 6/21/46, p7. 550w

Baker, John. *The Capture of Makin.* Washington, D.C.: War Department Report, 1946. 136p

The battle on Makin as told by Baker and the men who fought there.

Balchen, Brent. *War Below Zero: The Battle for Greenland.* Boston: Houghton Mifflin, 1944. 127p

Picture of daily living and working endured by fighting men on duty near the frozen Arctic where "a deep breath will shrivel your lungs." The publisher's note explained that "in the summer of 1941, an expedition led by Colonel Brent Balchen, veteran flier and explorer, sailed under secret orders for Greenland. Their mission was to establish the northernmost American air base in the world. They discovered that the Germans already had a weather station there in daily communication with Berlin. This station Colonel Balchen's men destroyed May 25, 1943." Other incidents related several air crashes on the frozen ice caps.

NYT 6/18/44, p3. 320w

WBR 7/2/44, p2. 750w

Baldwin, Hanson. *The Navy at War: Paintings and Drawings by Combat Artists.* New York: Morrow, 1943. 160p

Baldwin's commentary amounts to a brief naval history of the early years of the war, supplementing the pictures of five talented artists charged with the job of illustrating in drawing and paint the various experiences of navy men in action. Good as wartime history as well as art.

BW 1/16/44, p6. 380w

NYT 12/26/43, p9. 550w

Bank, Bertram. *Back from the Living Dead: The Infamous Death March and Thirty-Three Months in a Jap Prison.* Tuscaloosa, Ala.: privately printed, 1945. 108p

In the book, Bank describes his capture, imprisonment, liberation, and return to the United States after nearly three years of suffering in a Japanese prison camp. (Bank is the man identified as "Captain Bert of Alabama" by Colonel Dyess in his own account of the same Death March experience, entitled *Dyess Story.* Later Dyess led a successful prison break with other men that Bank was too ill to join.) This account actually begins at the end of Bank's ordeal describing his rescue by a contingent of American Rangers and Filipino guerrillas after heavy fighting against a strong garrison of Japanese soldiers. The rest of the book graphically describes the whole experience: the denial of food and water during the long five-day trek to camp; men who dropped from fatigue being bayoneted and left to die at the side of the road; fingers cut off to get rings; Filipino civilians being killed for secretly giving food to prisoners; prisoners killing dogs and cats for food to prevent starvation; dysentery as a universal plague in the camp. While sadistic guard brutality was common, there were rare exceptions. Bank, in fact, tells of one decent Japanese guard "who was so good . . . never known to have hit an American. . . . He told me that he liked the Americans but that Roosevelt should be killed, then the war would be over." Bank concluded this account with the curious remark that "he had been given the same propaganda about Roosevelt that we [Americans] have been given about Hitler."

Banning, Kendal. *Our Army Today*. New York: Funk & Wagnalls, 1943. 359p

A firsthand account of the world of army camps and military training in the United States by Banning, who delivers a report that, according to the book's foreword, is "a popular survey of the army, with emphasis on its equipment and the training of soldiers for mechanized combat, insofar as military regulations allow it to be told, with the conclusion that 'the Army today is better than publishable descriptions of it can reveal.'" A unique chapter explains how psychologists judge draftees' fitness for duty.

WBR 12/26/43, p10. 550w

Barker, John. *The Flight of the Liberators: The Story of the 454th Bombardment Group*. 1946. 172p

Cherished memories of the laughter, tears, and friendships that the members of the 454th shared. Stories about the clerks, mechanics, cooks, truck drivers, ordnance men, pilots, and turret gunners, from privates and sergeants to flight officers who participated in the bombing missions over Europe during World War II. This is the story of one group out of many, from activation and training to combat and "Bombs Away" ending with "Mission Accomplished." More than 100 photographs and a list of the 243 targets destroyed by the 454th from February 8, 1944, to April 25, 1945. Ultimately this is a tale of hundreds of young men who "lived hard . . . played hard . . . worked hard . . . fought hard," and felt a particularly precious closeness to one another through serious days and silly nights.

Barsis, Max. *They're All Yours, Uncle Sam!* New York: S. Daye, 1943. 103p

A collection of sketches with simple text related to women in the services, their training as Waves and Wacs, and the different perspectives revealed when they changed their civilian outfits for military uniforms.

BW 9/19/43, p4. 180w

WBR 10/31/43, 180w

Bartek, John, and **Austin Pardue**. *Life Out There: A Story of Faith and Courage*. New York: Scribner's Sons, 1943. 117p

One of three accounts (the others were the best-selling *Seven Came Through* by Eddie Rickenbacker and *We Thought We Heard the Angels Sing* by James Whittacker) recounting the experience of a group of men who spent twenty-one days on a raft drifting aimlessly on the vast Pacific Ocean after having survived a plane crash. The emphasis in this version was on Bartek's Bible reading as a source of hope. Remembering something his mother once said, that "you're going to get . . . in trouble sometime and you're going to have to depend on somebody higher to pull you out of it," Bartek trusted in the deliverance of prayers: "If two or three men gather together in the same place and believe the same thing and pray about it, then God will be there." His entire narrative of events underscored the religious aspects of their survival.

BW 6/6/43, p7. 500w

Christian Science Monitor 6/30/43, p13. 420w

Batcheller, Tryphosa. *France in Sunshine and Shadow*. New York: Brentano's, 1944. 202p

The story of a concert singer's escape from Paris and her survival after Nazis occupied the city. What comes across is a portrait of a woman of independent character who refuses to be intimidated by the threatening presence of the German conquerors.

WBR 5/14/44, p12. 200w

Bayler, Walter. *Last Man off Wake Island: A First-Person Narrative Told to Cecil Carnes*. Indianapolis, Ind.: Bobbs-Merrill, 1943. 367p

An account of the Wake Island fight against superior Japanese forces by an expert radio technician sent to install communications on the American base there. Aside from being the last free American to leave Wake Island before it fell, Colonel Bayler participated in other historic battles at Midway and Guadalcanal, making a record of American heroism against a determined enemy. A complete roster of the First Marine Battalion that fought on Wake Island is included.

NYT 5/2/43, p3. 1100w

WBR 5/9/43, p2. 1000w

Beattie, Edward. *Freely to Pass*. New York: Crowell, 1942. 372p

A record of the impressions of an American journalist, who from September 3, 1937, to January 7, 1941, covered and wrote about the

Sino–Japanese conflict (from Shanghai), the Nazi takeover of Czechoslovakia (from Munich), and the German invasion of Poland (from Warsaw). Later, as a war correspondent accredited to cover the British Expeditionary Force on the Continent, he witnessed the collapse of France under the Blitzkrieg.

> *NYT* 11/1/42, p5. 900w

————. *Diary of a Kriegie.* New York: Crowell, 1946. 312p

The diary of an American newspaper correspondent who was captured by the Germans during the American sweep through France. Contains not only details of prison camp life in Lemberg, Berlin, and Luckenwalde, it also offers impressions of the moral and military disintegration of the Third Reich leading to the ultimate Nazi collapse.

> *NYT* 4/14/46, p4. 340w
> *WBR* 3/3/46, p6. 1100w

Beck, L. C. *Fighter Pilot.* Huntington Park, Calif.: Privately published, 1946.

Story of the glorified life of one of America's young men, from birth to his parachute jump when his plane became disabled over enemy-held France. Lt. Beck managed to evade capture and remained for some days sheltered in hiding by sympathetic French citizens, during which time he wrote of his experiences and placed his notes in safe hands. Eventually arrested by the Gestapo in Paris, he was imprisoned not as a POW but as a political prisoner, and died in a concentration camp.

Beecher, John. *All Brave Sailors: The Story of the SS* Booker T. Washington. New York: L. B. Fischer, 1945. 205p

Written by the great-great-nephew of Harriet Beecher Stowe, this account tells the story of the first of four U.S. ships to be commanded by an African American. Although the navy was dubious about entrusting a cargo vessel to a "negro," two major factors—the shortage of able-bodied seamen and pressure from various advocacy groups—overcame any resistance. After the ship made her first difficult trip across the submarine-infested Atlantic, the "experiment" was deemed a success. The book is made up of sketches about the fine cooperation that existed among the mixed black and white crew, "one of the few spots in all the American war effort that isn't Jim Crow, where Negroes and Whites and men of all races and nations get the chance to show they can really work altogether in harmony."

> *NYT* 8/26/45, p24. 270w
> *WBR* 8/19/45, p7. 600w

Belden, Jack. *Retreat with Stilwell*. New York: Knopf, 1943. 368p

Exciting adventures of an American war correspondent during the fighting in Burma against invading Japanese forces. Along with notes on politics and propaganda, there are vivid descriptions of the destruction of oil wells, a raging fire at Mandalay, distraught native civilians caught in the battles, and the flight across Burma to India of a small remnant of soldiers and Burmese nurses led by American "Vinegar Joe" Stilwell.

> *SRL* 3/1/43, p7. 1250w
>
> *WBR* 3/7/43, p31. 2800w

————. *Still Time to Die*. New York: Harper, 1944. 322p

Episodic, somewhat disjointed account of Belden's experiences in battles that took place in China, North Africa, and Italy, along with his reactions to them. In a series of vignettes, Belden describes war's "dumb bestial suffering in all its stark ugliness and terrible obscenity." His rhetoric is somewhat impressionistic, with an approach that is more artistic than reportorial.

> *NYT* 9/17/44, p3. 1300w

Bell, Edith. *Adrift*, as told to J. H. Hunter. Grand Rapids, Mich.: Zondervan, 1943. 96p

Story of 20 days adrift on an 8'x10' raft in the south Atlantic. Mrs. Bell, her two children, and 14 other survivors from a torpedoed ship ran the gamut of emotions as they endured heavy seas, sharks, sun and saltwater sores, bloated hands and feet, and dreary exhaustion. Hunter writes that "the story is [told] for one purpose only, and that is to illustrate the faithfulness of God who said, 'Call upon me in time of trouble and I will deliver thee.'"

Bell, Frederick. *Condition Red: Destroyer Action in the South Pacific*. New York: Longmans, Green, and Co., 1943. 274p

Commander Bell of the pseudonymic U.S.S. destroyer "G" tells of battles in and around the Java Sea, the Coral Sea, and Guadalcanal. With a prevailing lustiness and fair amount of good humor, the author describes and analyzes the psychological patterns of what men think and how they behave as members of the least celebrated branch of the naval fleet.

> *BW* 12/19/43, p4. 700w
>
> *NYT* 1/2/44, p7. 600w

Bennett, John. *Letters from England*. San Antonio, Tex.: Hertzog, 1945. 136p [100 copies printed]

Air force officer tells of bombing missions to Norway, Germany, and elsewhere. It is more a running account by Bennett with photographs, covering his "confused" and "very" anxious feelings not only about his "first combat mission" but others as well, especially over the "Happy Valley"—so called because of the greatest "concentration of [enemy] anti-aircraft guns." Bennett admits that "we were all afraid," but that despite the heavy losses suffered on each raid, their courage never faltered. There are some interesting descriptions of a small English village near to where "American Aerodromes" were built, a battle-scarred London, an unscarred Paris, the thousands of misplaced peoples of the Continent when war ended, and Frenchmen, Belgians, even Hungarian, Austrian, and German soldiers wandering the roadsides of Europe "trying to find their way back to what was once their homes."

Bennett, Lowell. *Assignment to Nowhere: The Battle for Tunisia.* New York: Vanguard, 1943. 316p [100 copies printed]

Bennett's comprehensive view of the Tunisian campaigns, including comments on the political and diplomatic aspects of the war in that theater of operations, along with descriptions of civilian life in North Africa. Although the narrative possesses some historic value, the serious matters of the moment become somewhat vitiated by breezy commentaries.

> *NYT* 6/20/43, p.3. 950w
> *WBR* 7/11/43, p6. 1500w

———. *Parachute to Berlin.* New York: Vanguard, 1945. 252p

The author, an INS correspondent, went on a raid over Germany with the RAF. The trip proved to be a one-way affair, as Bennett parachuted to German soil, was captured, and spent some time escaping and being recaptured, until he was finally released from a concentration camp by the arrival of the Russians. Writing for *Weekly Book Review*, Marcus Duffield remarked, "Bennett's conclusions as to the results of air warfare and the Allied claims of strategic bombing deserve consideration."

> *BW* 11/25/44, p16. 600w

Bernstein, Walter. *Keep Your Head Down.* New York: Viking, 1945. 213p

Bernstein's book is made up of a series of articles, previously published in the *New Yorker*, dealing with his army experiences from 1941 to 1944. After lengthy descriptions of army training in the States, Bernstein recounts the fighting in Sicily and Italy's mainland and an overland march with fifty partisans in Yugoslavia. The chapter titles offer guidance to the contents; among them, "Action in Georgia," "The Taking of Ficarra," "I Love Mountain Warfare," "March 3, Tito's Headquarters."

> *NYT* 5/6/45, p3. 1000w
> *WBR* 5/6/45, p2. 800w

Berry, Robert. *Gunners Get Glory,* as told to Lloyd Wendt. Indianapolis, Ind.: Bobbs-Merrill, 1943. 293p

Berry's is a tale of a little-known and little-glorified branch of the service, highlighting the sacrifices and achievements of the regular navy men who "ride shotgun" on cargo vessels, manning the anti-sub and antiaircraft guns over seas threatened by enemy U-boats and planes, all the while serving as goodwill ambassadors among the civilian sailors of the merchant service.

BW 1/2/44, p3. 550w

NYT 12/26/43, p8. 440w

Biddle, George. *Artist at War.* New York: Viking, 1944. 241p

The author–artist produced an illustrated war diary covering his eight months spent with American troops in Tunisia, Sicily, and the Italian mainland. The twofold effect of drawings and text made the war and the men who fought it more understandable to the folks back home, conveying what the ordinary soldier experiences in his exhausting battles with the enemy, as well as war's inevitable human and material destructiveness.

NYT 11/16/44, p3. 1450w

SRL 1/29/44, p9. 1350w

————. *War Drawings.* New York: Hyperion, 1944. 78p

With 12 pages in full color and approximately 100 drawings, each with captions, this book is a kind of companion to Biddle's *Artist at War.* The illustrations once again convey what the artist felt war to be like: its overwhelming weariness at times, its personal sense of desolation, the misery and despair felt by the men who did the fighting.

NYT 1/21/45, p12. 550w

WBR 12/24/44, p3. 400w

Binder, Jenane. *One Crowded Hour: The Saga of an American Boy.* New York: Frederick Press, 1946.

Story of airman Lt. Ted Binder, "master of a good German accent, the archetype of Nordic blond, acquainted with the terrain of northwestern Europe and the workings of the Underground, with long experience in camping in the Wisconsin woods, plus a strong physique," which should have fitted him for eventual survival when his B-17 was shot up and he had to bail out over enemy territory. These are notes from a diary he kept while in hiding in various places, undiscovered when he was apprehended by the Gestapo.

Blackford, Mansel, ed. *On Board the USS* Mason: *The World War Diary of James A. Dunn, 1944–1945.* Columbus: Ohio University Press, 1996.

After early resistance to recruiting African Americans into the regular navy, except as stevedores in the Sea Bees, a more enlightened policy opened up opportunities for African Americans such as James Dunn, who served as a regular signalman along with 160 other enlisted seamen—black and white—and 44 white officers assigned to the destroyer-escort *Mason*. From June 1944 through May 1945, Dunn kept a daily log of his life on board, recording the *Mason*'s wartime activities from the first convoy it shepherded across the Atlantic to the end of the war. Aside from routine accounts of attacking enemy submarines and the long days of boredom during slow and tedious convoy passages, Dunn exhibited a political awareness of the groundbreaking exploits of the *Mason* crew, specifically referring to the fact that blacks and whites "worked good together just like a machine, smooth most of the time."

Bonnell, John. *Britons Under Fire*. New York: Harper, 1944. 178p.

A personal narrative with a religious perspective by a Presbyterian minister from New York describing what he saw and did during a trip to war-torn England in the summer of 1941.

> *Books* 1/11/42, p19. 170w

Bonney, Therese. *Europe's Children, 1939 to 1943*. New York: Plantin, 1943. 64p

Photographs of starving children, with emaciated bodies and distended bellies, make this an effective pictorial tract against the horrors of war. With brief accompanying text, the purpose of Bonney's book is an argument for shipping food to enemy-occupied countries in Europe, mainly for the salvation of "the little people" who are tragic victims of war.

> *Commonweal* 11/26/43, p147. 310w
> *NYT* 3/26/44, p8. 480w

Booker, Edna, and **John Potter**. *Flight from China*. New York: Macmillan, 1945. 236p

The book is divided in two parts, the first where Booker (Mrs. Potter) describes the exotic atmosphere of life in 1920s and 1930s Shanghai, including a chronology of old and new political developments before the Japanese occupation. The second part—written by John Potter—discusses Japanese policies in Shanghai after Pearl Harbor, then tells of his experiences in a Japanese prison camp. Neither of the Potters suffered or witnessed any of the atrocities which other prisoners elsewhere reported.

> *SRL* 9/8/45, p12. 700w
> *WBR* 8/26/45, p5. 700w

Brady, Alice. *Children Under Fire*. Los Angeles: Columbia, 1942. 192p

Story of the U.S. Committee for the Care of Children caught in the path of the Nazi war machine in Holland, Belgium, and France, as well as the threat to the children of England. Under the auspices of Alice Brady, hundreds of British and Continental children were shepherded to safety across the Atlantic. There are graphic portraits of British families living through German aerial bombardments, told in a series of daily journal entries from June 26, 1940, to June 1941.

Breger, David. *Private Breger's War: His Adventures in Britain and at the Front*. New York: Random House, 1944. 241p

Cartoons with captioned commentaries depicting how the war affects a worried army private who had difficulty understanding what it was all about. He "comforts" himself with the conviction that the war and his being in the army are temporary sidings off the main rail line of life. Breger's is a more nonsensical and funny view of the army contrasted to the somber cynical one presented by Bill Mauldin's Willy and Joe in his *Up Front*.

BW 4/2/44, p9. 230w

WBR 3/16/44, p4. 450w

————. *G.I. Joe*. (Private Breger). Garden City, N.Y.: Blue Ribbon Books, 1945. 96p

The continuing humorous history in cartoons and captions selected from those previously printed in *Yank* and *Stars and Stripes*, showing G.I. Joe at the front.

BW 4/9/45, p10. 310w

Brereton, Lewis. *The Brereton Diaries*. New York: W. Morrow, 1946. 450p

General Brereton, an Annapolis graduate, offers, in a mix of official communiqués and technical data, a good deal of information about the use of airborne troops in army units. While there is nothing new in this, there is much that is of historical value provided by an officer who worked in every theater of operation from October 3, 1941, to May 8, 1945, serving under both MacArthur and Eisenhower in Java, Australia, India, Egypt, North Africa, England, and France.

NYT 10/13/46, p6. 1300w

WBR 9/29/46, p1. 1800w

Briggs, David. *Action Amid Ruins*. New York: American Field Service, 1945. 124p

A down-to-earth mass observer commentary by an ambulance driver who tended the wounded during the bitter fighting in North Africa and Italy, comparing the war in the desert with the war in Italy, where in one there are no displaced civilians, no bridges, no dams, or cultural monuments at risk: "If a bomb or a shell opens a hole in the desert floor, the wind and drifting sand filled it in again," but in a land like Italy, ancient buildings and modern infrastructures suffer much destruction.

Brines, Russell. *Until They Eat Stones.* Philadelphia: J. B. Lippincott, 1944. 340p

Part of the book describes how the author, an American correspondent, and his family were trapped when the Japanese took Manila. After a time spent in an internment camp, they were allowed to return home on the hospital ship *Gripsholm.* Not only does he recount his prison camp experiences as such, he offers his impressions of the Japanese religious and cultural predilections that fueled their war aims.

NYT 1/14/44, p 1. 1200w

WBR 1/7/44, p5. 1300w

Brink, Ebenezer. *And God Was There.* Philadelphia: Westminster Press, 1944. 92p

Personal reminiscences of a chaplain serving with the troops in North Africa. One reviewer (*Book Week* 5/10/44) summed up the sense and substance of the minister's report as "a story largely based upon his experiences in the African-Tunisian campaign. The incidents are not unusually spectacular and not nearly as dramatic as some of the better known stories of men on life-rafts or in fox-holes. . . . Some of them are probably such that the men themselves would not re-tell them, but, cumulatively, they indicate the pattern which, irrespective of man's personal religious and racial loyalty, would evidence the discovery of a great abiding faith in God."

Brock, Ray. *Nor Any Victory.* New York: Reynal & Hitchcock, 1942. 351p

A personal narrative in dialogue form detailing the experiences of a *New York Times* war correspondent during the two years he covered the fighting in Yugoslavia and parts of the Near East. Brock tells of the Serb defiance against the Nazis' attempt to subjugate people he had come to know and appreciate for their courage to resist and strike back at the enemy invaders every chance they got.

Books 12/6/42, p4. 1040w

NYT 12/27/42, p5. 850w

Brown, Cecil. *Suez to Singapore.* New York: Random House, 1942. 545p

What an American radio commentator witnessed in the war zones from the Near to the Far East. Aside from his report on the sinking of the *Prince of Wales* and the *Repulse,* and some jungle skirmishes in the South Pacific, the part of the book that would be interesting to most historians is the well-documented revelations of blunders and mistakes committed by top echelon military and civilian officials in North Africa and Singapore. A reporter's objectivity is infused with anger at the incompetence he witnessed in high places.

NR 10/16/42, p 550. 1200w

NYT 10/25/42, p3. 1350p

Brown, David. *Marine from Virginia*; letters, 1941-1945. University of North Carolina Press, 1946, 105p

A collection of letters written by Marine Lt. Brown to various friends and family members, beginning in July 1941, and detailing training in the United States and thereafter recounting several battles in the Pacific, until March 1945, just before he was killed in action—about which a fellow Marine said, "He was always thinking of others and never of himself, and I cannot but think this philosophy of his was somewhat responsible for his death." The letters are filled with a mix of feelings and thoughts: At one time he wished he could "have about six weeks at home then return [to the war] for one or two more years! That is the commonplace dream of men overseas." He was convinced "that this is Thomas Jefferson's war—the war of the Common Man against tyranny . . . a war for democracy and not for power or materialism." In another letter, Brown explained, "Expressions of patriotism are misleading . . . in a sense that I do not fight for that multitude of states spread over the continent. I fight for these secondarily, in the sense that we fight for our allies, and for the cause of all free peoples. But we could never do that with true and generous sympathy, if we did not fight for our homes, first and last. And home is a narrow thing if profound." And in one of his last letters he admitted that "once or twice through places like Peleliu . . . all of us feel the reality of death in a new way . . . one half of us . . . keenly alive, the other half quite gone into that land of shadow—which is also destined to be ours [and that] when we see how quickly good men fall, it is plain as day to see all that's left. That *this* life is the shadow not the other."

Brown, Ernest. *The War in Maps: An Atlas of the* New York Times *Maps*. New York: Oxford, 1942. 159p

A collection of maps illustrating both the political and military aspects of the war. Useful to laymen and experts, the wide coverage is arranged for easy reference, with brief textual notes explaining and amplifying the purpose of the maps. Complementary to the daily newspaper coverage and radio reports of the battles being fought on all the war's diverse fronts. Good pictorial and textual aids to a global overview of the campaigns being waged against enemies in the four corners of the earth.

NYT 12/13/42, p8. 360w

SRL 11/21/42, p2. 420w

————. *The War in Maps: An Atlas of the* New York Times *Maps.* New York: Oxford, 1944. 167p

An updated history in maps with comments about the war (to 1944) being waged all over the globe.

NYT 11/5/44, p2. 420w

Brown, Harry. *Artie Greengroin, Pfc.* New York: Knopf, 1945. 212p

By the author of *A Walk in the Sun*, a serious novel about war on the bloody battlefields of Italy, these sketches appeared for the value of their humorous look at war in *Yank*, the army weekly. Most of Brown's caricatures depict Artie Greengroin, a typical American private, stationed in Britain, "alternately bored, astonished, delighted and depressed by what he saw about him." The best episodes show Artie in the guardhouse, at the movies, waiting to meet a duchess, cooking Spam and brussel sprouts, or talking about sergeants, ditch-digging, and war weariness.

NYT 7/15/45, p5. 1100w

WBR 7/15/45, p2. 800w

Brown, James. *Russia Fights*; with a foreword by Ambassador Joseph E. Davies. New York: C. Scribner's Sons, 1943. 276p

Along with Brown's reactions to a convoy battle in the North Atlantic and descriptions of his correspondent colleagues in Moscow, he provides a good factual picture of the sacrifices the Russian people made as they resisted the German army within their borders.

NYT 8/1/43, p10. 700w

SRL 7/17/43, p7. 800w

Brown, Joe E. *Your Kids and Mine.* Garden City, N.Y: Doubleday, 1944. 192p

A Hollywood movie star of the 1930s writes of his travels entertaining troops on the battlefields around the world. Sentimental and hard-hitting in turn, he describes the ordinary soldier at war in much the same twofold manner—with grins on their faces despite the weight of the world on their shoulders. Having lost a son in the fighting, Joe E. Brown writes with feeling and a personal accent that brought the awful sadness of war home to all those families whose loved ones were at risk.

Commonweal 12/15/44, p236. 310p

NYT 11/25/44, p10. 440w

Brown, John Mason. *To All Hands.* New York: McGraw, 1943. 236p

"The pieces that comprise the book were written to be spoken as daily broadcasts to the fifteen hundred soldiers and sailors aboard the flagship of the amphibious force that formed part of the Sicilian invasion. Lieutenant Brown was bridge announcer and his job was to use the ship's public address system to talk to the men every day about what was going on aboard ship and, as much as could be told, what was going on throughout the convoy and on all the fighting fronts to boot" (*New Yorker*). Generously illustrated with official navy photographs and watercolor sketches of action, Brown's reporting becomes a conventional mixture of jokes, topical references, quotations from Shakespeare and Matthew Arnold, official communiqués relating to the war and politics on battlefronts around the world, and news about the other elements of their convoy-armada sailing toward its D-Day-H-Hour mission of the plan to invade Sicily. Throughout all this, Brown shares with his shipmates his personal understanding of the imperatives for which they are forced to fight, which he summarizes (in chapter 26) as the "inhuman conduct of the enemy against Jews, priests, liberals in their own and heretofore neighboring countries."

NYT 11/7/43, p3. 1850w

WBR 11/7/43, p1. 2000w

————. *Many a Watchful Night*. New York: McGraw-Hill, 1944. 219p
Illustrated with photographs and reproductions of paintings, this second personal narrative by the former Broadway drama critic somewhat duplicates the role he played in *To All Hands*, as bridge announcer on a navy ship, this time as part of the amphibious force that was to support the D-Day landing on the Normandy beaches. Part of the book is a record of experiences somewhat removed from the war, such as a description of London by moonlight and a visit with George Bernard Shaw, the preeminent Irish playwright. Still, the book is a valuable resource for the impact of war on the minds and feelings of American soldiers and sailors during the long months of preinvasion preparations in England and during the first days of fighting on the Continent. The book ends on an extremely personal and cautionary note, declaring that no matter how triumphant this first step on the long road to ultimate victory, and the hopes of freedom and peace which it raised, those hopes, he asserted solemnly, can only be realized when nations seek rational solutions to their grievances other than war, and "men . . . learn to live at least as well as they now know how to die."

NR 1/45, p26. 1250w

Brown, Wenzell. *Hong Kong Aftermath*. New York: Smith and Durrell, 1943. 283p
A personal report of British and American men, women, and children who were captured by the Japanese when Hong Kong fell and

existed in prison camps suffering brutal treatment and all manner of privations at the hands of the conquerors.

   NYT 8/8/43, p7. 1100
   SRL 8/14/43, p17. 400w

Bulosan, Carlos. *Voice of Bataan.* New York: Coward-McCann, 1944. 29p

Poems that reveal the emotions of the soldiers who fought where defeat was victory. In one piece he writes: "The winds of hope cry out their names; the Heroes / Who fighting, lived their lives over again; dying / They became immortal among the dead."

   SRL 11/4/44, p23. 140w

Bunker, John, ed. *The SIU at War.* New York: Seafarers International Union of North America, 1944. 47p

True experiences of the war at sea involving members of the Seafarers International Union. "To the Persian Gulf and the Barents Sea; to the wreck-strewn Caribbean and the far reaches of the Pacific, men of the Seafarers, International Union have sailed the cargoes of war. Hundreds of them have made the supreme sacrifice along the sea routes to the fighting fronts. Salerno, Guadalcanal, Bari, Bizerte, Murmansk; these names, too, are memorials of their courage, for there and in other ports, SIU men delivered the goods only to die at their posts on fighting freighters. In three years of war nineteen hundred men of the Seafarers International Union have died in the line of duty; on the torpedoed ships, on blacked-out vessels sunk in collisions; in engagements with enemy surface raiders, in storms, and in air attacks. Countless stories could be told of their courage, fortitude, and resourcefulness; stories fit to rank with the best annals of the sea. But may the few included here be a memorial for them—a tribute to this legion of the SIU who gave their lives in the fight for freedom" (preface). Replete with tales of unarmed ships without convoys, men braving the submarine menace alone, many ships sunk, many men adrift for days in lifeboats and on rafts, episodes of fire fighting among barrels of gasoline and explosives, and men jeopardizing and even sacrificing themselves so that shipmates might live. Poetry included in the little book says it all:

> You are the prey of the U-Boat pack
> That lurk on the Ocean's Merchant track
> Your hulls lay blasted on the ocean's bed.
> While your sister ships sail overhead.

> She was laden deep with goods of war
> Below her marks both aft and fore
> And as if to tempt the hand of fate
> Her decks were piled with plane and crate.

Why, there's not a cargo great or small,
But a Liberty Tramp has carried them all,
High test gas and TNT
From Guadalcanal to Tripoli.

The Murmansk run, and Attu's shore,
Salerno beach-head and many more,
After the Naval gun-fire shook,
You were the first to drop your hook.

Burman, Ben. *Miracle on the Congo*. New York: John Day, 1942. 153p

Burman, an American novelist, tells a story that is part contemporary politics and part literary rhetoric. His report of a trip across Africa to Egypt possesses some documentary relevance, marred by long stretches of what can only be described as "travelogue literature" sprinkled with tom-toms, crocodiles, and romantic Dark-Continent mystery.

NR 7/27/42, p123. 1150w

Burns, Eugene. *Then There Was One: The USS* Enterprise *and the First Year of War*. New York: Harcourt, Brace, and Co., 1944. 179p

An account of the experiences of the navy flyers attached to the carrier *Enterprise* during the first year of the war. The "Big E" played a major role in every naval action in the Pacific, with the single exception of the Coral Sea battle, and Burns, an Associated Press correspondent who lived aboard the *Enterprise* for nearly five months, gives a careful factual report of the exploits of the men who discharged their hazardous duties with great honor. Much of the book, however, is based on hearsay and consequently the writing either assumes a quality of romantic fiction or lapses into patriotic exuberance.

BW 5/14/44, p3. 600w

NYT 5/28/44, p28. 480w

Busch, Noel. *My Unconsidered Judgment*. Boston: Houghton Mifflin, 1944. 196p

A collection of articles by a *Life* magazine editor offering his impressions of the geography, life, economics, and history of several countries he traveled to during the war: Ireland, England, South Africa, Egypt, Saudi Arabia, and Argentina. In the end Busch makes the odd remark that the best way to abolish war is to begin by abolishing peace in the postwar world!

NYT 7/16/44, p5. 1300w

WBR 7/23/44, p4. 700w

Butcher, Harry. *My Three Years with Eisenhower: The Personal Diary of the Naval Aide to General Eisenhower, 1942 to 1945; Captain Harry C. Butcher, USNR.* New York: Simon & Schuster, 1946. 911p

A great source of supplementary political and military history of World War II involving the top echelon of the Allied military and diplomatic officials. Butcher's appealing portrait of "Ike" balances Ralph Ingersoll's expressed criticism of the American general in his own personal narrative, *Top Secret.* According to the prominent historian, Arthur Schlesinger Jr., Butcher challenges Ingersoll's assertion that Eisenhower was simply a British stooge. The portrait outlined in this long book ought to be of particular value for Eisenhower biographers. Excellent photographs and a month-by-month summary of the war's progress in both theaters are included.

Nation 5/25/46, p629. 1550w

NYT 4/24/46, p1. 1800w

Caldwell, Cyril. *Air Power and Total War.* New York: Coward-McCann, 1944. 244p

A survey of the part air power played in World War II, including arguments for and against the justification for bombing civilian centers, whether in London or Berlin. He concludes that air power "appears to be the ascendant force and that it will prove to be the most decisive factor" in the present war and in future conflicts.

BW 8/8/43, p9. 500w

WBR 8/15/43, p10. 1150w

Caldwell, Erskine. *All-Out on the Road to Smolensk.* New York: Duell, Sloan, and Pearce, 1942. 230p

An early eyewitness account of the fighting in Russia, written by the author of an important 1930s documentary, *You Have Seen Their Faces,* done in collaboration with Margaret Bourke-White, the renowned photographer and author of her own wartime personal narrative, *They Called It "Purple Heart Valley."* Caldwell's report covers the German air raids on Moscow as well as resolute and committed fighters battling the Nazi invaders near Smolensk, victorious incidents which verified Soviet propaganda claims.

Nation 3/4/42, p316. 900w

NYT 3/1/42, p3. 600w

Campbell, Alfred. *Guadalcanal Round Trip: The Story of an American Red Cross Field Director in the Present War.* Lambertville, N.J.: Privately printed, 1945.

Foreword by Richard Tregaskis (*Guadalcanal Diary*). The story of a civilian Red Cross director in World War II which details the conscientious efforts of a noncombatant who helped in many ways to bring a brand of diversion and cheer to the troops on their way to battle —supplying them with playing cards, checkerboards, movies, boxing gloves, even fishing tackle—to both ease the boredom of a rendezvous voyage to a staging area and relieve the tense anticipation about an approaching assault.

Cant, Gilbert. *War at Sea.* New York: John Day, 1942. 340p

An account by the *New York Post*'s news supervisor of the struggle to safeguard the overseas shipping lanes from belligerents. Highlighted are many sea battles in the early war years, including a report of the courageous action of a tiny Dutch flotilla during the invasion of the Netherlands. Sound scholarship is indicated by the number of statistical tables that complement running accounts of hostilities.

> *Books* 3/15/42, p2. 950w
>
> *YR* Summer 1942, p841. 800w

————. *America's Navy in World War II.* New York: John Day, 1943. 452p

A continuation of the author's *War at Sea* (1942), the book describes the naval actions in the Mediterranean, the Atlantic, and the Pacific, including the loss of the USS *Chicago* off Guadalcanal. Official communications and eyewitness accounts enhance the narrative, making the report a valuable source for historians. Especially moving are the many tales of official citations for gallantry.

> *YR* Winter 1944, p356. 1300w
>
> *WBR* 8/2/44, p5. 1300w

Carlisle, John M. *Red Arrow Men: Stories about the 32nd Division on the Villa Verde.* Detroit: Arnold-Powers, 1945. 215p

This is a collection of stories about the Villa Verde campaign in the Philippines during the summer of 1945. According to the author, a civilian reporter who spent many long weeks covering the fighting over the mountainous terrain of Northern Luzon, "Nowhere in the history of World War II was the American soldier called upon to show more daring and head-on bravery than GI Joe . . . against a determined, fanatical enemy" (preface). Carlisle's is a firsthand witness account of the "red arrow boys" facing defenses prepared by the Japanese general infamously known as the "Tiger of Malaya" and the "Butcher of Bataan." Along with episodes of heroic actions against enemy troops hidden in caves and concealed pill boxes, there are chapters which celebrate the human qualities of nurses and medics caring for the wounded on the battlefield, generals who shared frontline foxholes with ordinary soldiers, combat engineers building roads "with the Japs banging away at them." In much the same manner of Ernie Pyle's earlier war narratives, Carlisle personalizes every incident, from moments of high tension at the front to quieter times in the rear, by identifying those who served in the campaign by name, rank, and hometown. While Carlisle had been a firsthand witness to the 119 grueling days of American gallantry and sacrifice, echoing observations registered by many other battlefield correspondents, he remarked, "It occurred to me again and again that while true democracy was fighting to preserve its way of life, GI Joe was fighting to get home."

Carlson, Alvin O. *He Is Able: Faith Overcomes Fear in a Foxhole.* Grand Rapids, Mich.: Zondervan, 1945. 82p

This book focuses on the faith-strengthening experiences the writer, as a military chaplain, shared with men in battle. "It is the author's earnest prayer that Christians everywhere may experience a dynamic revitalization of their faith in the God of the foxhole, the rubber raft, and the cockpit" (preface). Chaplain Carlson tells of several incidents where men under an enemy barrage of shot and shell cried with fear but conquered it through "the power of Christ." A typical declaration by one soldier represents the comforting assurance of religious faith that sustained many of his comrades: "You know, Chappie, I was so scared . . . that I thought I'd die without getting hit, but somehow I just held onto faith and prayer and I made it." Others not so lucky were fortunate in another way, in that according to the author they had looks "of untold confidence [as they] left this life to be with Christ [their] Saviour." Throughout, including an analogous reference to the celebrated experience of Eddie Rickenbacker, where "Seven Came Through" after drifting 24 days on life rafts in the wide Pacific, he recounts episodes of men petrified by fear of dying who come to believe that faith in God "would deliver them." At the same time, Chaplain Carlson was ready to allow that "not all men pray in times of danger [but] curse rather than pray." However, determined to counter the glib argument that "there are no atheists in foxholes," and the equally cynical notion of "foxhole conversation" that would have no lasting influence in the faith of servicemen after the war, he nevertheless maintains a strong conviction that those who really "entered into the 'faith of reality' will remain faithful" after the foxhole fear is a worry of another time and place.

Carmer, Carl. *The Jesse James of the Java Sea.* New York: Farrar & Rinehart, 1945. 119p

The manuscript of this book, originally entitled *Stars Fell on Alabama*, had its publication held up by navy censors in 1943 without explanation. When Carmer's narrative was finally allowed to be published, it had evolved from a strictly factual account into a semi-fictional history of the activities of the submarine *Sturgeon* during its missions in the China and Java seas immediately following the Japanese attack on Pearl Harbor, ultimately sinking thousands of enemy cargo vessel tonnage. The monotony of long stretches of undersea duty is duly noted.

> *BW* 1/13/46, p320. 480w
>
> *WBR* 1/6/46, p8. 600w

Carroll, Gordon, ed. *History in the Writing*. New York: Duell, Sloan, and Pearce, 1945. 401p

Disconnected dispatches by the foreign correspondents of *Time*, *Life*, and *Fortune* reporting the events in the European and the Pacific war zones. William Long, Jack Belden, and Robert Sherrod are a few of the reporters who contributed to its pages, themselves having published book-length narratives of their own firsthand experiences covering various aspects of the war. Some of the dispatches attempt to characterize what the young men on the fighting fronts felt, others to analyze home-front moods in wartime.

> *NR* 9/10/45, p320. 480w
>
> *WBR* 8/5/45, p18. 600w

Carroll, Wallace. *We're in This with Russia*. Boston: Houghton, 1942. 264p

A record of the author's visit to Russia in the autumn of 1941, wherein he describes the courage and stoic endurance of the Russian people at war, with illuminating interviews and human portraits. British and French diplomacy preceding the German invasion of Russia comes in for some criticism.

> *Current History* 1/43, p453. 580w
>
> *NYT* 10/4/42, p4. 1250w

Carse, Robert. *Unconquered: Europe Fights Back*. New York: R. M. McBride, 1942. 225p

In separate chapters, Carse tells somewhat similar stories of individuals, some of whom appear to be semi-fictional, from different countries occupied by the Nazis, everyone sharing the same suffocating predicament of curtailed liberties and all manner of oppression. In each land, there is a resentment against the invaders by ordinary folks in small ways and a growing underground of organized resistance. The suffering and struggles of peoples of Holland, Belgium, Norway, France, Greece, Yugoslavia, Czechoslovakia, Poland, and even fascist Spain are highlighted.

> *Books* 12/20/42, p99. 800w

————. *There Go the Ships*. New York: W. Morrow, 1942, 156p

A seaman's story of an Arctic convoy. The author, formerly a newspaper reporter, shipped aboard a merchant vessel on a trip carrying supplies to Russia from the United States. His book records the experiences of that long dangerous voyage across the North Atlantic, around the northern end of Norway to Murmansk—a voyage beset by fog, ice, and storm, German submarines, enemy raiders, mines, and dive bombers. Added to these potential disasters was the fact that Carse's ship carried tons of high explosives, easily ignitable, which could send all hands to the frigid waters of the Arctic Ocean. At the same time, in *There Go the Ships*, Carse reported the extent of the contributions and sacrifices made to the war effort by a ragtag complement of ABS (Able-Bodied Seamen) and the frightful cost of unsung lives lost during every crossing. The sailors who manned the "lifeline" were not many—less than one hundred thousand—compared to the number of uniformed troops, but by 1944 more than four thousand had given their lives. "Sinkings of Allied shipping as I write this are at a sickening rate. My guess is that at least three thousand seamen every month are having their ships blown out from under them. Some of these guys are picked up. But not all of them."

   Books 12/6/42, p5. 1350w
   NYT 12/6/42, p2. 1100w

————. *Lifeline: The Ships and Men of Our Merchant Marine at War*. New York: W. Morrow, 1943. 189p

The story of the American merchant marine at war, describing the ships, the men who ran them, and their deeds of heroism while keeping the sea lanes open. In addition, Carse provides information to anyone who might be considering becoming a merchant seaman.

   NYT 1/30/44, p12. 600w

Cartwright, Reginald. *Mercy and Murder: An American Ambulance Driver's Experiences in Finland, Norway, and France*. London: Iliffe & Sons, 1941. 86p

A volunteer American ambulance driver's experience in Finland, where he endured "machine gunning and bombing . . . from Soviet planes" and being strafed while with the Finnish ski patrol, followed by a second tour of duty in Norway and France, describing other wartime horrors and tragedies, this time being bombed and shot at by the Germans, causing him to comment ultimately that "it is not encouraging to hear . . . radio recitals of further atrocities by the Hitler Regime . . . or to the make-up of German youth there . . . grafted [with] an utterly savage strain. . . . If Britain wins, Hitler and Co. will not wait to be rounded up; they will disappear as already arranged. If they are caught the judiciary appointed by civilization would give them short shrift. If they win they will lose because mankind never marks time and God in his Heaven is just."

Casey, Robert. *I Can't Forget: Personal Experiences of a War Correspondent in France, Luxemburg, Germany, Belgium, Spain, and England.* Indianapolis, Ind.: Bobbs-Merrill, 1941. 399p

Reports of the early months of the so-called phony war and vivid pictures of the people in those war-torn nations and the tragedies and heartbreaks suffered. A wandering, occasionally wayward, chronicle of the early skirmishes between the Germans and the French and the retreat to Paris and the south, which is a large and significant part of the book, all with a mixture of bitter sympathetic bemusement.

> *Books* 11/16/41, p16. 750w
>
> *NYT* 11/16/41, p4. 1400w

————. *Torpedo Junction: With the Pacific Fleet from Pearl Harbor to Midway.* Indianapolis, Ind.: Bobbs-Merrill, 1943. 438p

In turns analytical, insightful, and humorous, Casey provides a sober and encouraging account of the transformation of the U.S. Navy from the disaster of Pearl Harbor into a considerable fighting force. His narrative, mostly in diary form, relates events involving successful naval operations from the Marshall Islands to the battles of the Coral Sea and Midway.

> *Books* 12/13/42, p14. 950w
>
> *NYT* 12/6/42, p3. 1050w

————. *Battle Below: The War of the Submarines.* Indianapolis, Ind.: Bobbs-Merrill, 1945. 380p

One of three submarine narratives that were suppressed, for inexplicable reasons, by the Navy Department in 1943, even though the navy itself had cooperated with the author in its preparation. Wartime censorship denied the reading public an informative report of the tales, legends, and grim routines of the men who fought the war from beneath the sea. The submarine experience—its terror and fascination—is vividly conveyed.

> *NYT* 8/18/45, p62. 1150w
>
> *WBR* 7/29/45, p3. 900w

————. *This Is Where I Came In.* Indianapolis, Ind.: Bobbs-Merrill, 1945. 307p

A veteran Chicago journalist summarizes five years of European war from a "truly personal" perspective. His impressions of the many ordinary and extraordinary people he had met, places he had been, and events that he had witnessed are filled with wit and a romantically generous spirit. As the war unfolded, he reports the retreat out of Paris, the endless bombing of London, the buzz bombs, the air war over Germany, the destruction of the Luftwaffe, the miracle of D-Day, the hecatomb of the hedgerows, and the scientific massacre of Von Rundstedt's Seventh Army.

SRL 9/8/45, p28. 450w

Cassidy, Henry. *Moscow Dateline, 1941–1943*. Boston: Houghton Mifflin, 1943. 375p

A correspondent for the Associated Press writes a professional report on the wartime events in Russia, detailing the battles for Moscow, Sevastopol, and Stalingrad objectively. Cassidy's book makes a real contribution to the historical record with his accounts of the meetings between Stalin, Churchill, and Wendell Wilkie as well as the Japanese Foreign Minister, Matsouka, who had just signed a nonaggression pact of friendship with the USSR. Cassidy's opening comment, however, takes credit for the prescience which could only come from hindsight when he declared that "everyone except those who should know, realized (in the spring of 1941) that the two greatest powers of Continental Europe, Russia and Germany, were about to come to grips."

WBR 5/30/43, p3. 1300w

Cave, Hugh. *Long Were the Nights: The Saga of the Squadron "X" in the Solomons*. New York: Dodd, 1943. 220p

An account of torpedo boat warfare in and around Guadalcanal. The story of PTs engaging elements of the Japanese South Pacific fleet reveals a good deal about the men and the peculiar problems involved in this unique kind of hit-and-run fighting for which these quick and maneuverable boats were built. For example: "Night after night [the boats] had hit the enemy hard and then fled back to their base, leaving Jap ships in distress behind them burning, sinking ships on which men were . . . hurt and killed." The material Cave accumulated, based on the words of the men who served deadly missions in the most vulnerable of navy crafts, duplicative of White's *They Were Expendable*, evoked proud appreciation for the PTs' pivotal role in America's first serious offensive. Cave's narrative offered a David vs. Goliath story: The navy credited these light "Squadron X" mosquito boats with the sinking of a heavy cruiser, six destroyers, a submarine, and two or three small ships.

NYT 1/16/43, p23. 700w

WBR 1/2/43, p3. 1150w

———. *We Build We Fight! The Story of the Seabees*. New York: Harper & Brothers, 1944. 122p

A story of the navy's construction battalions, describing the work of the steam shovel men, bulldozer operators, dynamiters, linemen, divers, steel workers, carpenters, blacksmiths, mechanics, and others. Their work is outlined at Guadalcanal, in the Solomons, Bougain-

ville, the Aleutians, Iceland, and Salerno. Illustrated with official
United States Navy photographs.

>   *Kirkus* 6/15/44, p280. 160w

Chaplin, William. *Seventy Thousand Miles of War: Being One Man's
Odyssey on Many Fronts.* New York: Appleton-Century, 1943. 287p

From the "phony war" to the evacuation of the British army at Dunkirk and the fall of France, Chaplin journeys to cover events in India, Egypt, and Moscow. Somewhat anecdotal in its attempt to create a sense of wartime life in far-off lands, occasionally taking on the quality of a travelogue, it is nevertheless a valuable record, by a skillful witness, of events of the critical early years of the European war.

>   *SRL* 12/11/43, p30. 500w

————. *Fifty-Two Days: An NBC Reporter's Story of the Battles That
Freed France.* Indianapolis, Ind.: Bobbs-Merrill, 1944. 215p

An eyewitness record of the first 52 days of fighting on French soil after D-Day—June 6, 1944. He describes the tall glider poles the Nazis erected in the open fields to impede airborne Allied troops, and the cost in dead and wounded Americans storming concrete enemy pill boxes and block houses with flamethrowers, leading to an eventual breakout of the beachhead on the first day. Aside from historical battles being fought and won, Chaplin offers telling glimpses of how American GIs felt about the job they were sent to do.

>   *WBR* 12/3/44, p30. 500w

Chernoff, Howard. *Anybody Here from West Virginia?* Introduction
by Edward R. Murrow. Charleston, W.Va.: Charleston Publishing Co.,
1945. 105p

Interviews with soldiers conducted by a war correspondent whose purpose was to act as a conduit of information about servicemen to the folks back home. Through his reports, a few GIs get a chance to "talk" to loved ones, in the process allowing the morale of the whole outfit to improve. A typical example of the many stories reported: "Attention all Logan girls: Private Gordon A. Potter is now out of circulation. He is married to an Irish girl and hopes to bring her back to Logan after the war." Chernoff sums up his approach by comparison: "Most of the correspondents over here are bent on one thing—that is covering the war. I'm going to leave that to the news services and the major networks while I tell you some of the little known things."

Childs, John. *Navy Gun Crew.* New York: Thomas Y. Crowell, 1943.
111p

Account of regular navy sailors assigned to man guns fitted on merchant freighters as they cross the Atlantic in convoys constantly threatened by German U-boats. It details the routine and work of the gunners from the time they ship out until the convoy reaches safe harbor.

> *Library Journal* 9/1/43, p672. 90w

Chunn, Charles. *Of Rice and Men: The Story of Americans under the Rising Sun.* Los Angeles: Veterans Publishing Co., 1947. 230p

A record of the experiences of Americans "in a Nip prison." The material for the book was collected as a "morale project in Colbonatuam Prison Camp #1 in 1942, [providing] an outlet to the ambitions of writers and artists incarcerated." Included are sketches, poetry, and personal diaries that tell how prisoners were "clubbed . . . kicked and shot." An endnote by Chunn reveals his bitterness toward the brutal treatment the prisoners received: "Although the names and races and peoples are usually capitalized, we feel that japs and formosans (taiwans) are sub-human and therefore should be common—and contemptible—nouns."

Clare, Thomas. *Lookin' Eastward: A G.I. Salaam to India.* New York: Macmillan, 1945. 320p

A personal narrative made from a collection of letters written by a U.S. Army chaplain to his wife over a two-year period of service with the 341st Bomber Group in India, before he was reported missing in a plane crash. In his letters he tells of conversations he had with the men of the squadron, revealing how they felt about India and how they behaved while there.

> *SRL* 7/14/45, p8. 310w
> *WBR* 5/13/45, p14. 450w

Clark, Thomas. *Remember Pearl Harbor.* New York: Modern Age, 1942. 127p

Writing in *Books*, March 22, 1942, one reviewer summed up the content of Clark's narrative this way: "Mr. Clark's slender but informative volume tells his own experiences on the day of the raid, of the initial incredulity of people that the bombs falling on Pearl Harbor could be real, of the completeness of the Japanese surprise in all parts of the island. He tells of the bravery under fire of everyone, service men and civilians alike, of the fortitude of the wounded, of the blood donors lining up at the hospitals, eager to do what they could. He indicates the reactions of the Japanese population, during and after the raid, and the effective help which the loyal Japanese are giving in ferreting out traitors."

> *NYT* 3/15/42, p13. 480w

Clausen, Walter. *Blood for the Emperor: A Narrative History of the Human Side of War in the Pacific.* New York: Appleton-Century, 1943. 341p

Clausen, as Associated Press correspondent, wrote stories gathered from participants in all branches of the service, even including a penetrating analysis of enemy soldiers. In addition, he tells of various Japanese espionage activities in Honolulu and secret enemy agents being signaled to from Japanese submarines off the coast of Hawaii. After nearly two years of war, Clausen concludes, "the Japanese goal of drawing the white man out of the Orient has been achieved. [The enemy now] has the rubber and the tin and aluminum that we lack. All that she needs now is time to develop these resources."

> *SRL* 9/11/43, p23. 600w

Claypool, James. *God on a Battlewagon*. Philadelphia: John C. Winston, 1944. 110p

Based on a series of articles, first published by the *Chicago Tribune*, reporting the role of a navy chaplain in keeping the morale high of the sailors on the fighting ship *South Dakota*, encouraging the men to "Fight the Good Fight," and setting a courageous example himself through two hard battles against the Japanese. Typically, he served the religious needs of the men by conducting Mass and Holy Communion services, teaching Bible classes, and leading hymn singing, along with ceremonies for the burial at sea of the fallen. An exemplar of a militant holy man, Captain Claypool became known as "the fighting Parson."

Coale, Griffith. *North Atlantic Patrol: The Log of a Seagoing Artist*. New York: Farrar & Rinehart, 1942. 48p

Reproductions of sketches and paintings done by Coale in his official duty as artist with the North Atlantic fleet. Some of the pictures include depictions of the mountainous seas and perilous rescues, the mud of Newfoundland, and the cliffs of Iceland.

> *Books* 7/19/42, p4. 3800w
>
> *NYT* 7/19/42, p1. 900w

———. *Victory at Midway*. New York: Farrar & Rinehart, 1944. 178p

The author, attached to the navy as an artist, was given the assignment to represent the war on canvas and murals. Reproductions of his painting and sketches on the Pearl Harbor attack and episodes of the Battle of Midway, with commentaries, are collected in this book.

> *BW* 3/26/44. 500w
>
> *NYT* 2/20/44, p7. 900w

Coffin, Howard. *Malta Story: Based on the Diary Record of His Experiences with the Sample Pages of the Coffin Diary*. New York: E. P. Dutton, 1943. 222p

This is a factual story with a fictional gloss of experiences of an American pilot who joined the Royal Air Force in January 1941 and served on British-held Malta during more than a year of heavy enemy air and sea attacks. While it is a true story gleaned from Flying Officer Coffin's diary, detailing the relentless bombing by the Germans, the loss of RAF pilots, and chronic shortages of trained replacements, planes, and food, there is a novelistic quality to the book, especially with its interludes of love stories involving Coffin and others with Maltese women.

> *BW* 8/1/43, p1. 900w
> *WBR* 7/25/43, p1. 1700w

Colonna, Jerry. *Who Threw That Coconut!* Garden City, N.Y.: McCombs, 1945. 94p

Comedian Colonna gave servicemen, according to Bob Hope, "a chance to relax and enjoy a mental furlough from the job of taking on" the Japanese, when he entertained the troops on the battlefronts of the South Pacific. In a compilation of the madder aspects of the trip, he tells of baseball games on Guadalcanal, movies shown in a jungle, goofy hours on a bomber, wisecracks under fire. It adds up to the reflections of a zany, silly man and a deep-thinking, serious person. Filled with sensational large drawings by Sig Vogs.

Connelly, Kenneth. *Chaplain's Assistant*. Seattle: Craftsman Press, 1945.

Sketchy sidelights of army life, tracing a soldier's days from a training camp in the South, across the Atlantic to England, then on to France, Belgium, Holland, and finally Germany and victory. Corporal Connelly details his actions, comporting himself under enemy fire in such a way that his highly commendable behavior proved to be a definite morale builder for his comrades (who experienced some of the heaviest fighting in the war). A model of faith, Connelly emphasized the spiritual and moral power that made an Allied victory possible.

Cook, Don. *Fighting Americans of Today*. New York: Dutton, 1944. 191p

Popularly written, biographical sketches of Dwight D. Eisenhower, Mark Wayne Clark, George Patton Jr., William F. Halsey Jr., Alexander Archer Vandegrift, Clare L. Chennault, George C. Marshall, Ernest J. King, Henry H. Arnold, and James H. Doolittle.

Cooke, Elliot. *All but Me and Thee: Psychiatry at the Foxhole Level*. Washington, D.C.: *Infantry Journal Press*, 1946. 215p

A report on the serious loss of manpower and the fighting ability of soldiers because of psychoneurosis disorders. General Cooke, charged with a mission to research the subject, toured military bases all over the United States, England, and North Africa, conducting interviews with anyone who had experience with the problems and could suggest ways to handle them. The book has many recommendations to make about how the army should deal with psychoneurosis in the ranks.

Kirkus 10/15/46, p532. 270w

SRL 12/21/46, p14. 850w

Cooper, Page. *Navy Nurse*. New York: McGraw-Hill, 1946. 226p

The work, the hardships, and the adventures of trained nurses on duty with the navy in various battle zones around the world, from the Aleutians to New Guinea, from the Philippines to Ireland, taking care of casualties—and a few who spent years in the filth of Japanese prison camps.

NYT 3/17/46, p10. 320w

WBR 2/17/46, p28. 600w

Corkin, Frank. *Pacific Postmark: A Series of Letters from Aboard a Fighting Destroyer in the War Waters of the Pacific*. Hartford, Conn.: Case, Lockwood, and Brainward, 1945. 172p

Corkin's letters to a small hometown newspaper tell not only his story, but represent the stories of thousands of other young men in the war, which helped the families to see, through his eyes, what their sons and husbands were meeting up with. Much talk, in between shore bombardment and sub-chasing action, of movies, popular singers, natives on Micronesia, haircuts, the tragedy of the five Sullivan boys lost in action, strikes at home and their effect on the servicemen ("it's about time people began thinking about increasing the size of the Army and Navy instead of the size of their own pocket book"), with the one word *loneliness* summing up the effect the war had on everyone. In his final letter Corkin wrote how he helped a navy chaplain conduct a funeral service for a sailor recently killed.

Cowles, Virginia. *Looking for Trouble*. New York: Harper, 1941. 447p

The memoirs of an American woman journalist who covered most of the important European events of the late 1930s. Her book tells of her experiences in Spain during the civil war, of visits to Russia, Germany, Prague, and Paris before and after Munich, and her observations of English courage during the summer and fall of 1940. Vivid depiction of a "nosey" American newspaper woman "looking for trouble" in the explosive environment of Europe from 1935 through the worst of the London blitz in 1940.

Crane, Aimée, ed. *Marines at War*. New York: Hyperion. 1943. 128p

Watercolors and pencil drawings, oil, and pen-and-ink sketches from 19 artists vividly depict battles in the Pacific, revealing both the vulnerability as well as the toughness of the young marines (average age, 19+) who did not necessarily understand the war needs but understood the needs of each other with a fierceness that is both unsettling and comforting, which these visualizations make evident.

NYT 11/28/43, p3. 700w

WBR 12/12/43, p1. 500w

Crawford, Carl. *Salvage Diver.* Hollywood, Fla. William-Frederick Press, 1946. 80p

Recounts episodes of salvage divers at work and play in southern France, North Africa, and the Azores, emphasizing the camaraderie of the men who do dangerous work, and telling of the equipment (the usual gear: insulated watertight suits, 35-pound lead-soled shoes, a 60-pound helmet, air bags, etc.) and slipping into the sea with underwater welding tools to disentangle lines caught in propeller shafts, inspecting sunken vessels, setting dynamite charges to wrecks, opening harbors to traffic, occasionally encountering booby-trapped sunken ships, and even enduring an octopus embrace.

Crawford, Kenneth. *Report on North Africa.* New York: Farrar & Rinehart, 1943. 206p

In the spring of 1943, Crawford spent three months as a reporter assessing the political and military situation which the Allies faced in their efforts to dislodge Axis presence on the African continent. His conclusion is that the British–American decision to adopt the lines of military expediency and power politics was the only viable one. Large portions of the book provide useful facts on the economies of North African countries.

Nation 10/16/43, p449. 1450w

NYT 10/17/43, p7. 1450w

Crawford, William. *Gore and Glory: A Story of American Heroism.* Philadelphia: David McKay, 1944. 192p

The personal experiences of Captain Crawford, an American flyer during the first year of combat against the Japanese in the Pacific, when the United States was outnumbered on the ground, in the air, and on the sea. Despite handicaps of limited resources, the young pilot of a Flying Fortress, "scared to death, but eager to do his job," recounts a series of hair-raising adventures, including a raid on a convoy bringing reinforcements to a Japanese garrison in New Guinea during which the entire flotilla of enemy ships was destroyed. Once, during a frightening battle, his Fortress suffered bullet and flak damage so severe the plane was never fit to fly again.

Cudahy, John. *The Armies March*. New York: Scribner, 1941. 304p

A former American ambassador to Belgium when the war in Europe started, Cudahy, hired by *Life*, returned to Germany to write on the social, political, and economic realities of the Third Reich, the survey of which became the substance of this book. Included in his report are interviews with Hess and Hitler and an analysis of the German national character.

Books 12/21/41, p11. 800w

Curtiss, Mina, ed. *Letters Home*. Boston: Little, Brown and Company. 1944. 310p

A collection of letters written by World War II servicemen to friends and families—their words transport readers from Hometown, U.S.A., to every distant outpost in the four corners of the globe. Truly personal feelings expressed by young Americans suffering every kind of discomfort while facing possible death with quiet bravery. The themes run the gamut of the soldiers' potential: patriotic, daring, resourceful, cheerful, understanding, homesick, worried, reassuring.

SRL 7/8/44, p13. 900w

Time 6/17/44, p99. 1750w

Custer, Joseph. *Through the Perilous Night: The Astoria's Last Battle*. New York: Macmillan, 1944. 243p

A disjointed, censor-handicapped report on the cruiser *Astoria*'s last battle, a night action off Savo Island near the coast of Guadalcanal, where on one disastrous night it was sent to the bottom by enemy action. Correspondent Custer, having suffered an eye injury while onboard, devotes many pages to the medical treatment received by him and other wounded men.

SRL 8/24/44, p23. 500w

Daniell, Raymond. *Civilians Must Fight*. Garden City, N.Y.: Doubleday, 1941. 322p

Reminiscences of a *New York Times* correspondent in which he attempts to portray what civilian life is like in a country fighting for its existence against the most ruthless military power that has been seen in modern times. "It is not a diary or a textbook of civilian defense. It is rather an account of ordinary life in London, both before and after the Blitzkrieg on England began." The early part of the book describes the routine of a correspondent's life in a wartime city. When the Blitz came to London, Daniell reports the reaction of the British people to the terrible ordeal. Of particular interest is a conclusion passed on to the American people—that the essence of a civilian defense against air raids is preparation.

Books 11/23/41, p7. 340w

NYT 12/7/41, p7. 800w

Dashiell, Samuel. *Victory Through Africa.* New York: Smith and Durell, 1943. 320p

A political perspective on events from the capitulation of France, the establishment of Petain's Vichy government, and the factional intrigues rampant in Algeria up until the time American forces landed in North Africa.

NYT 7/11/43, p6. 600w

WBR 7/18/43, p16. 1200w

Davis, Harry, ed. *This Is It!* New York: Vanguard, 1944. 22p

A collection of 12 brief stories of personal experiences by Americans who were involved in the actual fighting in various ways. Davis acts as an interviewer, gathering accounts from a chaplain, a pilot, a coastguardsman, a pharmacist's mate, among others, then turning their words into readable copy. At the same time, he maintains the flavor of the way these men normally spoke, avoiding embellishments or literary gloss.

BW 4/9/44, p9. 330w

NYT 4/16/44, p6. 460w

Davis, Hassolt. *Half-Past When: An American with the Fighting French.* Philadelphia: J. B. Lippincott, 1944. 283p

An American, Davis became an officer in the French army, keeping a diary of his experiences, which form the substance of his personal narrative. In a review published in the *New York Times* on January 28, 1944, the book is fairly summarized: "Mr. Davis has filled his book with descriptions of the flies, the insects and the filth he encountered; of the venereal diseases of the natives; of the most horrifying cruelties that man can inflict upon man; of brothels and prostitutes and all manner of other lurid matters . . . (told with a rather self-conscious toughness) which some readers may find colorful and others revolting."

WBR 12/17/44, p6. 460w

Davis, Kenneth. *Soldier of Democracy.* New York: Doubleday, Doran, and Co., 1945. 566p

The book covers the whole of the author's youth and manhood, down to the day he returned to his home in Kansas after the war. A somewhat one-sided, complimentary portrait of General Dwight D. Eisenhower emerges, although later historians might find much that is useful here, whatever more dispassionate perspectives they may bring to the subject.

NYT 12/9/45, p7. 1400w

SRL 12/1/45, p52. 1500w

Dealey, Ted. *Sunset in the East.* Dallas, Tex.: Privately published by the author's fellow workers of the *Dallas Morning News*, 1945. 65p

Dealey tells of "the greatest naval parade in history," as more than 80 battleships, cruisers, and destroyers that made up an armada of the United States fleet gathered in Tokyo Bay and other waters off the coast of a defeated Japan in September 1945. The main focus of the book is on the formal signing of the surrender documents aboard the USS *Missouri*, but some of the narrative tells the stories of rescued prisoners of war who had been, in utter disregard of the Geneva Convention rules, tortured and tormented while in captivity. In a scathing rebuke to the defeated enemy, Dealey offers a litany of grievances against the Japanese, reminding his readers of the horrors of the Bataan Death March and the bloody battles of Tarawa, Iwo Jima, and Okinawa that cost so much in American lives. Throughout, Dealey indulges in singularly negative references to the defeated "Japs," referring to them as "puny," inhuman "Nips," "bandy-legged," "pigmies," who were "half men," more like "chimpanzees in human clothing," assessing them as an "evil looking," "inferior race." The narrative concludes with a warm tribute to Ernie Pyle, the celebrated war correspondent, who was killed on Ie Shima, while covering the action of the 77th Division Infantry in battles near the end of the war.

Dennis, Clyde. *These Live On: The Best of True Stories Unveiling the Power and Presence of God in World War II.* Chicago: Good News Co., 1945. 204p

Ten thrilling stories from the world's battlefronts. Among the tales is the true story of Jake Armstrong, an all-American hero who found sudden death to be sudden glory in the Battle of Savo Sound, Guadalcanal. An epic tale of submarine warfare is another. The underlying focus of all the stories is the power of God in World War II.

Denny, Harold. *Behind Both Lines.* New York: Viking, 1942. 209p

Descriptions of desert warfare in North Africa similar in many ways to other reports of the same campaign. What is different in this narrative concerns the experience that correspondent Denny had when he was captured by the Germans in Libya. What he stresses about his time in Italian and German prisons is how decently he was treated, especially by the Italians, who often went beyond their duties to be friendly to him and others.

NYT 11/28/42, p3. 900w

Deutsch, Helene. *God Was with Me in a Japanese Concentration Camp.* Miami, Fla., 1945. 28p

A different kind of internment story, told by a daughter of missionary parents imprisoned when the Japanese army conquered parts of

South China. Moments of bad food and limited privileges were a small part of Deutsch's experience compared to the amount of freedom allowed to conduct religious classes and services. While the author recognized that other camps may not have been so lucky, "the Japanese decided to make ours a model camp and had a tennis court put in and an assembly hall for recreation," and even distributed yen, which along with money from the Swiss Consul each month enabled detainees to "buy Buffalo milk, fish on certain days, meat twice a week, eggs, vegetables . . . and some canned goods" at a store run by a Japanese couple. In time, Deutsch was among a number of other prisoners sent home on the exchange ship *Gripsholm*.

Dew, Gwen. *Prisoner of the Japs*. 1943. 304p

An American photographer–reporter arrested by the Japanese when they took Hong Kong, Dew spent six months in a prison camp before being released to return to America on the neutral Swedish hospital ship *Gripsholm*. Her account of this experience reveals, on the one hand, an admiration for the remarkably well-trained Japanese soldiers, and on the other her distress at their inexplicable cruelty (raping British nurses, disemboweling babies!).

NYT 1/6/43, p2. 1200w

WBR 6/20/43, p4. 1200w

Dewey, Albert. *As They Were*. New York: Beechhurst Press, 1946. 233p

In letters and excerpts from a journal kept by Lt. Colonel Dewey— who was killed during a raid—are thoughtful impressions of the early days of the war, and the reasons for the sudden collapse of the French army under the German blitzkrieg. Insights, sometimes mystical, sometimes informed, explain the way things were before the first German troops stormed across the borders in western Europe.

New Yorker 12/28/46, p65. 100w

Dickinson, Clarence, and **Boyden Sparkes**. *Flying Guns: Cockpit Record of a Naval Pilot from Pearl Harbor through Midway*. New York: C. Scribner & Sons, 1942. 196w

Cockpit records from Pearl Harbor through Midway of a pilot who had been recognized by the Navy Department as the fleet's outstanding combat flier. Lots of action, several brushes with death, a forced landing at sea, a parachute jump over mountainous terrain, rescues, interplane talk among fliers in battle: "Earl, you take the carrier on the left. Best, you take the carrier on the right"—samples of how quietly determined men act during moments of stress.

Nation 12/26/42. 196p

NYT 11/15/42, p6. 600w

DiPhillip, John. *Gunner's Diary*. Boston: Meador, 1946. 111p

The book is exactly what the title indicates, a diary written by a member of the U.S. Navy's Armed Guard assigned to merchant ships delivering supplies to Allied forces in Europe over an Atlantic Ocean teeming with enemy submarines. "The book deals mainly with the exploits of a gun crew serving aboard the USS *M. Flager*, an oil tanker owned by the Standard Oil Company. From the time it arrives in port after it has gone to sea, it relates the life and work of the Armed Guard, who protect the mighty ships while bringing across their precious cargo" (foreword). Most of the book describes the daily routine of life aboard such ships, filled with commonplace concerns about weather, food, sleep, preparatory drills, as well as an occasional brush with enemy subs, traveling in convoys to Ireland, Scotland, and back to North America. One particular entry describes what turned out to be a devastating submarine attack in which some 13 cargo ships, tankers, and troop transports were sunk. Once again, the author takes time to remind his readers of the truly democratic makeup of the men: "The crew were not all American, the gun crew being the only Americans, while the rest were a mixed crew, largely Danish, Swedish, Spanish, Cuban, and South American Negroes. Despite all our differences we were a proud crew and that's what made our ship a mighty one." For the most part, the *M. Flager* made its transocean runs without mishap, and "life seemed to roll calmly on board ship, for that we were grateful."

Donahue, Arthur. *Tally-ho: Yankee in a Spitfire*. New York: Macmillan, 1941. 190p

A young American from the Midwest who, at age 28 in the summer of 1940, enlisted in the British Royal Air Force as an experienced flier. Donahue provides realistic descriptions of what happens from the time the squadron assembles for a mission until its return to base. There are rousing descriptions of aerial battles along with the emotions a pilot feels under fire four miles up in the sky. Donahue also tells how he was shot down once, was wounded, but recovered to fly and fight again.

NYT 10/5/41, p5. 650w

———. *Last Flight from Singapore*. New York: Macmillan, 1943. 168p

An American flier serving with the RAF describes his emotions from combat briefings to bombing raids to safe returns to base. The book is made from a manuscript and photographs that were found among Flight Lt. Donahue's effects when he was reported missing after an attack on Japanese targets in the South Pacific.

NYT 1/9/44, p18. 550w

Donahue, Ralph. *Ready on the Right*. Kansas City, Kan.: Smith, 1946. 194p

A true story of a naturalist Seabee on the islands of Kodiak, Tanaga, MogMog, and several others, spending as much time or more between surveying duties for the Navy Construction Battalion exploring the animal life and digging for fossils, making notes on the bees, bugs, and birds found in these remote places of the Pacific region, collecting seashells, remarking on acrobatic ravens in Tanaga and the snowy white love terns on Ulitha's MogMog.

Dos Passos, John. *Tour of Duty*. Boston: Houghton Mifflin, 1946. 336p

Series of verbal snapshots, scenes from various theaters of war, some dealing with the Pacific bases and the Philippines, others with Europe, and comments ranging from admiration for the wartime spirit of America's citizen-soldiers to reports on Americans as administrators in Germany in the days of victory.

> *NYT* 8/25/46, p7. 1550w
> *WBR* 9/1/46, p2. 1135w

Douglas, John, and **Albert Salz**. *He's in the Merchant Marine Now*. New York: R. M. McBride, 1943. 224p

In a publisher's note, the book is said to be "an account of how apprentice seamen and merchant marine cadet-midshipmen are trained in wartime seamanship. . . . Here is described their life aboard and ashore, fighting back with anti-aircraft and machine guns, remaining at their posts until crippled ships limp into port."

> *SRL* 8/21/43, p25. 190w
> *Springfield Republican* 11/8/43, p8. 440w

Driscoll, Joseph. *War Discovers Alaska*. Philadelphia: J. B. Lippincott, 1943. 352p

Tells how American soldiers and sailors adjust to the vexations of cold, high prices, low numbers of women in the northern territory, sustained by a typical American sense of humor, clearly documented in the pages of the army newspaper *The Kodiak Bear*, which published anecdotes reflecting the serviceman's nearly congenital disposition to find the funny bone in most any uncomfortable situation. A more serious glimpse is reserved for acknowledgment of the important role played by prospectors from the U.S. Bureau of Mines tirelessly searching for strategic materials useful to the war effort.

> *NYT* 4/4/43, p6. 1050w
> *WBR* 4/11/43, p6. 1050w

————. *Pacific Victory*. Philadelphia: J. B. Lippincott, 1944. 297p

Experiences and observations of a war correspondent who covered news of the Pacific fleet for over a year, describing personalities from the highest ranking officers (Halsey, Nimitz, MacArthur) to the enlisted men in each branch of the service. A prevailing sense of humor accounts for the dogged and earthy anecdotes common to the fighting men, and a lack of reverence for the top brass among the men denotes for Driscoll something healthy about the American spirit.

> *WBR* 1/3/44, p1. 1050w

Dyess, William. *The Dyess Story: The Eyewitness Account of the Death March from Bataan and the Narrative of Experiences in Japanese Prison Camps and of Eventual Escape.* New York: G. P. Putnam's Sons, 1944. 182p

An eyewitness account of the "death march" from Bataan and a narrative of experiences in Japanese prison camps, including an eventual escape. Lt. Colonel Dyess' bitter account of the surrender of American forces and months of barbaric treatment at the hands of his Japanese captors.

> *BW* 4/30/44, p6. 550w

Eisenhower, Dwight. *Eisenhower's Own Story of the War: The Complete Report by the Supreme Commander General Dwight D. Eisenhower, on the War in Europe from the Day of Invasion to the Day of Victory.* New York: Arco, 1946. 122p

A document of historical worth by the Supreme Commander in Europe covering the day of the invasion to the day of victory. Especially interesting for its gracious assertions of the cooperative relationships between American and British commanders and troops. An example of "Ike's" intrinsic disposition of courtesy and statesmanship.

> *NYT* 1/32/46, p6. 900w
> *WBR* 8/11/46, p8. 750w

Eldridge, Fred. *Wrath in Burma: The Uncensored Story of General Stilwell and International Maneuvers in the Far East.* Garden City, N.Y.: Doubleday, 1946. 320p

A good picture of General Stilwell and the war in the China-Burma-India theater. Written by an American journalist who was "Vinegar Joe's" public relations officer, it is mostly a sympathetic portrait describing his defeat in Burma, suggesting that it was partially through the treachery of the Allies who created obstacles too difficult for the general to overcome. Personal animosity toward him displayed by the British, the Burmese, and the Chinese (especially by Chiang Kai Shek) is also seen as a contributing factor in Stilwell's defeat.

> *BW* 5/12/46, p2. 750w
> *Christian Science Monitor* 6/17/46, p14. 800w

Eldridge, Retha. *Bombs and Blessings.* Review and Herald, 1946.
Story of what it is like to be the Seventh-day Adventist missionary family of Retha and Paul Eldridge and their two children behind barbed wire in the Los Banos internment camp in the Philippines in the early days of 1945. "We were interns existing—not living—on mushy rice, and watery 'gravy.' Our forces had landed on Luzon, but uncertainty still loomed ahead of us. The days were swiftly passing, yet no thrilling news came of land action in our immediate vicinity. We [had] to endure the torturing suspense a little longer."

Ellsberg, Edward. *Under the Red Sea Sun.* New York: Dodd, 1946. 500p
The story of Commander Ellsberg's successful tackling of the awesome task of salvage, and returning to usefulness the shambled wreckage of the former Italian port of Massawa in Eritrea (raising sunken ships, rebuilding docks, etc.), despite the small complement of men assigned to the job, considerable red tape, and terrific heat. In an event such as war, where destruction is a virtue, the essence of Ellsberg's achievement was the restoration of a devastated facility to an efficiently operating service.

NYT 11/3/46, p5. 900w

WBR 11/3/46, p4. 1250w

Eustis, Morton. *War Letters of Morton Eustis to His Mother.* Washington, D.C.: Spiral Press, 1945.
The letters that are printed in this book were written by Morton Eustis, First Lt. U.S. Army, from February 6, 1941, to August 10, 1944. They cover the entire period of his army life—from training at Ft. Devens to three days before he was killed in action at Domforont, in Normandy. All of the letters were written to his mother with the exception of a few to other members of his family and friends. They were written with no thought of publication, although, as he said, he expected to use them as notes for a play or a book that he hoped to write after the war.

Exton, William, Jr. *He's in the Destroyers Now.* New York: McBride, 1944. 224p
Lt. Commander Exton explains the role of destroyers as part of the attack fleet operation in the Atlantic and Pacific theaters of war. In particular he details their support efforts for the North African landings.

Springfield Republican 4/20/44, p8. 120w

Flannery, Harry. *Assignment to Berlin.* New York: Knopf, 1942. 439p
Correspondent who spent 1940-1941 on assignment in Berlin reports the contemporary scene from inside Germany. Flannery deals

with the Nazi Press, sports and entertainment in the Third Reich, Hitler, Hess, and the early campaigns in Crete and Greece.

Nation 7/25/42, p78. 800w

New Statesman 10/10/42, p242. 1200w

Ford, Corey, and **Alastair Macbain**. *Cloak and Dagger: The Secret Story of the OSS.* New York: Random House, 1941. 216p

Experiences of members of the OSS (Office of Strategic Services) headed by General William "Wild Bill" Donovan during World War II, indulging in variety of clandestine activities behind enemy lines: setting up radio stations in Axis as well as occupied countries, printing and distributing bogus newspapers, training guerrillas, sabotaging enemy installations, rescuing downed Allied fliers.

NYT 2/24/46, p4. 1100w

SRL 6/15/46, p23. 800w

————. *The Last Time I Saw Them.* New York: Scribner, 1946. 216p

A log of the conduct, thoughts, and emotions of men who flew and serviced the planes that took off on combat missions from virtually every airfield around the world, from India to the Aleutians, from the warm South Pacific to icy Greenland in the North Atlantic, revealing the character of grave men apprehensive at briefings yet undaunted in battle.

NYT 5/19/46, p7. 900w

WBR 5/26/46, p2. 800w

Forgy, Howell. *"And Pass the Ammunition"*; edited by Jack Mcdowell New York: Appleton-Century, 1944. 242p

An intimate picture of life aboard an American warship by the chaplain of the *New Orleans*, describing his experiences at Pearl Harbor and later when his ship was badly damaged. In a mix of material as well as spiritual values, what Forgy calls "a very practical war" led him to conclude that "Christ was not an idealist; he was the world's greatest realist."

Christian Science Monitor 8/19/44, p12. 270w

NYT 8/20/44, p16. 460w

Forman, Harrison. *Report from Red China.* New York: Holt, 1945. 250p

The author, an American correspondent, reports that the Communists mobilized 100,000 peasants to fight the Japanese and were doing so, contrary to Chiang Kai Shek's Chungking assurances that they were not. Forman's view of the Chinese Communists differs markedly from those of the central government, creating what he concedes to be a seriously growing Chinese dilemma.

BW 3/11/45, p1. 1500w

NYT 3/11/45, p3. 2100w

Foss, Joe. *Joe Foss, Flying Marine: The Story of His Flying Circus.* New York: Dutton, 1943. 160p

The first part of the book tells about Foss' early life; later Foss provides a dramatic account of his war experiences as a Marine flier who achieved the status of "ace" for having shot down 26 enemy planes. The narrative is a testimony to the enterprise and courage not only of Foss but his many flying comrades.

    NYT 10/31/43, p40. 500w

    WBR 11/14/43, p4. 850w

Fox, Monroe. *Blind Adventure.* Philadelphia: J. B. Lippincott, 1946. 205p

The story of a navy man who was blinded when his ship received a hit in action against the enemy. The bulk of the narrative tells of Fox's hospital treatment and care, his convalescence and rehabilitation in the United States, finally detailing programs designed to make orientation back to civilian life easier.

    BW 9/15/46, p4. 390w

    WBR 8/18/46, p7. 1000w

Frank, Gerold, and **James D. Horan**. *USS* Sea Wolf: *Submarine Raider of the Pacific.* New York: Putnam, 1945. 197p

Joseph Eckberg, a radioman and sound-detection expert on the *Sea Wolf*, told to Frank and Horan his story of a year cruising above and below the sea, searching for and sinking or damaging many Japanese transports and fighting ships. Pointing to these successes, the authors draw attention to the ethnic and cultural mix of the crew in order to support the strength-in-diversity notion, contrary to the ethnocentric racial ideologies of both the Japanese and German adversaries.

    NYT 10/14/45, p17. 600w

    WBR 9/9/45, p8. 600w

Freeman, Charles Spencer. *One of Us Found the Way: Letters, Poems, and Selected Writings of Charles Spencer Freeman.* Dallas, Tex.: Wilkinson Publishing Co., 1946. 213p

This collection of the "beautiful" thoughts of Lt. Freeman was inspired by words he had written in September 1943, nearly 18 months before he was killed in action on February 1945: "The same bell will toll for all of us some day, and the reading of how it rang for theirs, how we lived and died, is something for posterity. We realize the importance of firsthand information, we in the Air Corps. . . . Any story of how people lived should be worth writing about." In this simple statement, Freeman explains for historians the value of all wartime personal narratives, including his letters (mostly written to his "Darling Mother") that detail his military odyssey as an

Air Force navigator from bases in the United States, then Bermuda, "where the British run around in long socks and short pants," to Algeria, Italy, and England.

Freeman, Don. *It Shouldn't Happen.* New York: Harcourt, 1945. 206p

In a series of illustrations, Freeman narrates the tale of an army private living a dog's life in camp who becomes through imaginative metempsychosis an actual dog recruit in the army K-9 corps. On the surface a humorous caricature of army life from a dog's view, there is, however, a lurking darkness around the whole business, which comes across as a grim allegory. It touched the raw nerve of one reviewer who declared that "*It Shouldn't Happen* is race propaganda, not just propaganda for racial justice. It is propaganda calculated to encourage bitterness and hatred—which is another thing altogether. Indeed, the final pages of Mr. Freeman's pictorial tract seem to suggest that justice is best achieved by violence. Since both white and black are also going to continue to live side by side in the post-war era, I don't believe this is much of a solution—rather quite the reverse."

NYT 8/24/45, p24. 80w

WBR 12/29/45, p67. 130w

French, Herbert. *My Yankee Paris.* New York: Vanguard, 1945. 260p

Experiences in Normandy and Paris described by an officer in the Quartermaster Corps who never felt the fear or even heard the noise of combat. Here is a view of the wartime life of one of the troops who lived comfortably, ate well, and slept in clean, warm beds. Filled with stories of French civilians and the fun side of army life in Paris.

NYT 12/2/45, p41. 270w

New Yorker 12/29/45, p67. 120w

Friedheim, Eric, and **Samuel Taylor.** *Fighters Up: The Story of American Fighter Pilots in the Battle of Europe.* Philadelphia: Macrae/Smith, 1945. 275p

Anecdotal and human interest stories of American Air Force fighter pilots in Europe from November 1943 through D-Day, describing the personal characteristics of some of the men, a few who became "aces." It also tells in vivid detail the immense amount of planning behind even a single flight of an unarmed reconnaissance plane over burning Berlin and of the vast and "intricate machinery of Air-Sea Rescue, which guided faltering planes home or fished out downed pilots from the Channel or the North Sea," in addition to typical fighting engagements against the Luftwaffe.

WBR 7/1/45, p10. 450w

Friendly, Alfred. *The Guys on the Ground*. New York: Eagle, 1944. 170p

A complimentary picture in a collection of articles and anecdotes by Captain Friendly about the ingenuity of "the guys on the ground." These are maintenance and repairmen who fix aircraft damaged in combat—seemingly headed for the junk heap—to make them fighter-worthy again. Feats such as reconstructing a patched aircraft from the wreckage of ten bombers and fighters were legendary. Indeed, the men on the ground had a better record for keeping planes operational under battle conditions than was the case of keeping civilian planes airworthy in peacetime. Putting the whole operation in perspective, Friendly points out that for every plane in the sky, there are 50 "men on the ground" who make battle sorties possible, from cooks to telephone operators, from construction gangs to all manner of clerks and liaison personnel.

WBR 8/15/44, p6. 600w

From Camp to College. *The Story of Japanese American Student Relocation*. Philadelphia: National Japanese American Student Relocation Council, 1945. 6p

According to the report, some 3,000 students of Japanese ancestry found their way out of Assembly and Relocation centers into more than 500 institutions of higher learning all over America—nearly all of the 2,500 Japanese students in West Coast colleges before Pearl Harbor having been given an opportunity to enhance their esteem.

Fry, Varian. *Surrender on Demand*. New York: Random House, 1945. 243

Tells of American activities from August 1940 to September 1941 (before the United States entered the war) on behalf of political and intellectual refugees being sought by the German Gestapo. As a member of the Emergency Rescue Committee, dealing with forged passports and an underground railroad across safe borders, Fry helped many doctors, painters, and writers to avoid Nazi dragnets.

NYT 4/22/45, p5. 1150w

WBR 5/20/45, p2. 1150w

Gallagher, Wesley. *Back Door to Berlin: The Full Story of the American Coup in North Africa*. Garden City, N.Y.: Doubleday, 1943. 242p

The author presents "the full story of the American coup in North Africa," a narrative valuable for its political notations rather than for its routine reports of armed clashes over vast stretches of endless desert, and stories of surprise air attacks, explosive death and destruction from enemy guns, even hand-to-hand combat. The most important part of the book focuses on the political wars being waged behind the lines among high-ranking military officers and assorted political diplomats. Also included is Gallagher's assessment of the complexities of dealing with Darlan and the Free French government in Algeria, along with a complimentary judgment on General Eisenhower's skill in coordinating the diverse interests of British and American strategists while managing to effect a consensus that ensured the Allies worked as a team for a common goal.

> *National Republican* 10/25/43, p581. 1200w
>
> *WBR* 9/26/43, p6. 1050w

Gannett, Frank. *Britain Sees It Through: A Report by Frank Gannett.* New Rochelle, N.Y.: Gannett Newspapers Publication, 1944. 44p

Tells of Gannett's visit overseas to American camps, airfields, British war plants, as well as his talks with Churchill and military leaders. Among several "tell-tale" chapters are: "How Britons Carry On," "The [US Servicemen] Need Letters," "German Morale."

Geer, Andrew. *Mercy in Hell: An American Ambulance Driver with the Eighth Army.* New York: Whittlesey, 1943. 264p

Geer, a former sparring partner of Jack Dempsey, served as a volunteer ambulance driver in the American Field Service Corps. During his 15 months' tour of duty with other volunteers he worked on the battlefields in the Tunisian campaign, tending the wounded and saving many lives. He concentrates on the gallantry of the men without guns who drove—often within sight of enemy lines—unprotected ambulances while battles raged. Geer took pains to remind readers that his story was less about himself and more a composite biography, a testament actually, of a unique group of men who, in their commitment to democracy's cause, risked ordeals from strafing enemy planes or a Panzer tank's exploding shells.

> *NYT* 7/25/43, p3. 900w
>
> *WBR* 7/11/43, p4. 11350w

Genovese, Joseph. *We Flew without Guns.* Philadelphia: Winston, 1945. 300p

This is the author's story of the many and varied experiences as a pilot with the Ferry Service of the RAF for a time, afterward flying passengers and cargo over the Himalayas from India to China. Genovese tells how "some guys want to win medals—some guys want to win wars," but the lure of adventure and high pay were primary motivations for what the regular army pilots considered "mercenary" service. Part of the reason he kept flying was the fringe benefit of beautiful Chinese girls and the most gorgeous courtesan in Calcutta fighting for his affection.

Gentile, Don. *One-Man Air Force*; as told to Ira Wolfert. New York: Graphic Enterprise, 1944. 55p

Details instances of aerial dogfights over Fortress Europe—what it takes to make a good fighter pilot, one who learned to become a confident killer without liking it much. Personal reflections about the enemy from an American "ace" who shot down 30 German planes and was dubbed "a one-man air force" by General Eisenhower. Speaking of his conquests over enemy fighters, Gentile said: "But suddenly, I don't know, something happened in their minds. You could see it plainly. Their brains had dissolved away under the pressure of fear and had become just dishwater. . . . They froze to their sticks," explaining that "German and American fighter planes are about the same. Maybe one has a little more speed, the other a little more maneuverability, but not much margin. So when the kids get into a fight it is a question of which is the better man."

    BW 8/27/44, p2. 100w

    NYT 8/13/44, p1. 1200w

Geren, Paul. *Burma Diary*. New York: Harper, 1943. 57p

In a recital of events that happened in Rangoon, Geren tells how Japanese air raids killed thousands of natives. The diary is chiefly a record of the author's stunned meditations and disturbed introspections on what he saw and felt as a witness to the tragic slaughter of so many innocent people.

    Crozer Quarterly 1/44, p89.

Gervasi, Frank. *War Has Seven Faces*. Garden City, N.Y.: Doubleday, 1942. 296p.

Reflections of a correspondent on what he saw, heard, and felt during and after a round-the-world junket to the principal newsworthy places on the globe—from England to the Philippines, South Africa and the Middle East, India, and Thailand to North Africa: these are the "seven faces" of a wartime season. After a review of past events, Gervasi offers predictions of what the future might hold.

    SRL 5/2/42, p10. 850w

    NYT 2/1/42, p3. 1050w

———. *But Soldiers Wondered Why*. Garden City, N.Y.: Doubleday, 1943. 267p

An account by an American journalist of a trip to South America and Africa in 1942. If the book's title suggests a lack of grassroots understanding of the reasons America and free peoples of the world were involved in a deadly conflict, there is little here testifying to such misgivings. In fact, the essence of Gervasi's disjointed accounts of people and places in the news is that "ordinary people" know "why" the threat of totalitarianism must be fought because "common people nearly everywhere . . . fundamentally believe in the same principles that resulted in the American [Bill of Rights]." At the same time, the author recognizes that there are still "antidemocratic European elements sniffing about [our] State Department," hoping to bring their baleful influence to the peace table.

WBR 8/15/43, p19. 1850w

Gibbs, Archie. *U-Boat Prisoner: The Life Story of a Texas Sailor.* Boston: Houghton, 1943. 208p

A true-to-life story with yarn-like qualities about a merchant seaman whose ship was torpedoed in the Caribbean and was soon fished out of the sea by the sympathetic crew of the German submarine that sank his ship. Gibbs tells of three days held in friendly captivity aboard the U-boat, how he was treated decently by the regular crew especially and his estimate of some of their lukewarm feelings about Hitler and Nazism, before he was transferred to a neutral Venezuelan motorboat and eventually put safely ashore. While the ostensible highlight of *U-Boat Prisoner* is the brief encounter with enemy sailors, the value of the book comes from the long biographical sketch about the years of his boyhood. Before the submarine episode, Gibbs tells the kind of story typical of documentary writers of the 1930s—about an impoverished family, a mother who went out of her mind from overwork, a father who abandoned his children to an orphanage or adoption, a 16-year-old Gibbs, who became a boy tramp among many victims of hard times, doing odd jobs, picking fruit, painting houses, loading freight. Finally, his aimless wandering took him to sea where, as an able-bodied sailor before and during the war, he voyaged to foreign ports around the globe. While the cosmos of a seaman's life and world culminating in the remarkable submarine visit is amply described, it is the larger cosmos of Depression America that affirms the book's documentary merit.

NYT 8/29/43, p4. 750w

WBR 8/15/43, p2. 950w

Gillmore, Margalo, and **Patricia Collinge**. *The B.O.W.S.* New York: Harcourt, 1945. 172p

Noted American actors Katherine Cornell and Brian Ahearne led a theatrical company on a tour of European camps, performing the Rudolph Besier play *The Barretts of Wimpole Street*, based on the romance between English writers Elizabeth Barrett and Robert Browning. Aside from the details related to the acting company's devotion to the play, there are recorded incidents of their relationships with the soldiers they met—their concern for the soldiers and the appreciation accorded to them by the men so far from home.

NYT 12/30/45, p5. 650w

Springfield Republican 12/30/45, p4. 500w

Gilroy, Maxwell. *Soldier of Misfortune*. Portland, Ore., 1945.

A humorous look at war, with many line-drawing sketches that graphically tell of army life: "Scars of mortal wounds inflicted upon our dignity, our pride, and our spirit. Only you and I know the scarring brand of the top-kick's wrath, on mornings we slept through reveille, and the lash of a mess sergeant's bellow cutting across our bare and glistening backs as we bent over the black and greasy pots in the blistering heat of a G.I. kitchen. We alone know the hate that a bugler can inspire at reveille, when the spirit's at its lowest ebb."

Glasser, Arthur. *And Some Believe: A Chaplain's Experiences with the Marines in the South Pacific*. Chicago: Moody Press, 1946.

Here is a record culled from letters written to his wife of how "in my own blundering way, I tried with God's help to 'keep at it' throughout my first tour of duty overseas." Details of Glasser's ministry as navy chaplain during an island assault, and the subsequent activities dealing with the muddy terrain, the jungle undergrowth, building roads, and repairing bridges, constantly determined to encourage men to maintain confidence in "God's Son, Jesus."

Goodell, Jane. *They Sent Me to Iceland*. New York: Washburn, 1943. 248p

Story of a Red Cross worker sent to Iceland to care for the morale of the servicemen stationed at a place General George Marshall called "one of the most nerve-wracking of American" stations, which took a special kind of courage by soldiers to endure. Goodell served many roles—cook, carpenter, secretary, nurse, housekeeper—in between arranging dances, concerts, and games of all kinds in a nearly forgotten outpost of constant rain, mud, and cold.

WBR 12/10/43, p10. 600w

SRL 2/5/44, p28. 600w

Graebner, Walter. *Round Trip to Russia*. Philadelphia: J. B. Lippincott, 1943. 216p

A *Time*, *Life*, and *Fortune* correspondent's record of days spent in the Soviet Union, reporting on some of the fighting but mostly concentrating on visits to collective farms, the war industry in the country, the daily lives of the people, Russian churches, and the ballet. Part of the narrative tells of the early phases of General Montgomery's Libyan campaign that he witnessed when he traveled home by way of North Africa.

Nation 5/1/43, p639. 900w

NYT 4/4/43, p8. 750w

Graham, Garrett. *Banzai Noel!* New York: Vanguard, 1944. 159p

Marine Captain Graham, a former World War I pilot known as a "retread," tells of his experiences on a ship bound for action on Guadalcanal and of the fighting, often with a morale-building sense of humor that enabled younger Marines to endure the incredible tensions of battle with the determination to do their best. Quentin Reynolds, the author of several personal narratives himself, remarked that "if the fates had dropped Mark Twain on the dreary island of Guadalcanal, this is the kind of book he might have written."

NYT 4/9/41, p16. 750w

Greening, C. Ross, and **Angelo Spinelli**. *How Our POWs Made "Little Americas" Behind Nazi Barbed Wire: The Story of the Yankee Kriegies.* New York: National Council of the YMCA, 1945. Unpaged.

Approximately 35 glossy sheets of text with some 70 informal photographs taken by prisoners, along with several drawings. "Much has been made of the hardships and privations suffered by American prisoners of war, but the world knows all too little of how the average prisoner, with typical Yankee ingenuity, daily achieved small miracles to ease the unfortunate lot for himself and his comrades" (introduction). This is the story of Americans coping, rendered through a series of brief alternating commentaries by Greening and Spinelli. In all, they tell of their experiences as prisoners of war from the moment of capture (a crash landing, a futile dash for freedom, and then the inevitable "For you der var ist ofver"). Greening tells how he managed to escape once and hide out for nearly nine months in Italy, eventually to be captured again. Spinelli remarks that "no camp ever had enough fuel, and we would strip pieces of wood from the barracks . . . trying to keep warm." There were plenty of organized sports—"boxing got a good [spectator] turnout." The theatrical bug bit some, resulting in amateur stage plays. Hobbies kept many men busy: wood carving, painting, repairing watches, even crafting a violin! Classroom programs were set up, covering lectures on "practical subjects which could be of help in civilian life . . . but there were classes in almost every high school or college course." Spinelli remarked that "next to food, I think, Kriegies thought more of escaping than anything else." But only a few tried, and rarely succeeded. At the end, Greening writes: "On June 2, after sixteen days at sea, we watched in reverent silence as the Statue of Liberty loomed out of the haze of a spring thunderstorm. I had nothing to say. . . . My heart was too full for words. . . . I had never fully realized before going overseas just how wonderful this country of ours is. I had always taken for granted my complete liberty, freedom of speech and countless luxuries that I considered my heritage as an American. . . . My year and a day of oppression and want in prison camp have changed my perspective completely. . . . I think I have learned my lesson well and feel that I shall never forget it. . . . I am an American! And I am grateful."

Greenlaw, Olga. *The Lady and the Tigers*. New York: Dutton, 1943. 317p

Story based on entries from Greenlaw's personal diary as well as official notes detailing the year when American volunteers fought for China and the viability of the Burma road. As the wife of the executive officer of Chennault's AVG, she tells what the war was like for the pilots known as the Flying Tigers, and their sorry treatment by the American army when the group disbanded.

NYT 9/5/43, p3. 850w

WBR 9/5/43, p5. 1300w

Grew, Joseph. *Report from Tokyo: A Message to the American People*. New York: Simon & Schuster, 1942. 88p

A blunt, sometimes passionate, description of military domination over Japanese international and domestic policies, all dedicated to Asian-wide conquests and the establishment of slave states under Japan's control. Based on a number of speeches made by the former ambassador to Japan, Grew's severe conclusion is that the Japanese ruling class and the country's military domination must be rooted out if peace is to be maintained in the Pacific.

American Political Science Review 4/43, p371. 3800w

NYT 12/13/42, p18. 100w

Griffin, Alexander. *A Ship to Remember: The Saga of the Hornet*. New York: Howell-Soskin, 1943. 288p

A chronicle of the aircraft carrier *Hornet* which ferried Jimmy Doolittle on his mission to bomb Japan early in the war (*see* Ted Lawson's *Thirty Seconds over Tokyo*), fought at the Battle of Midway, and assisted the Marines at Guadalcanal during their most difficult hours, before it was sunk by the Japanese.

NYT 12/12/43, p9. 700w

WBR 12/5/43, p3. 1550w

Griffin, Robert, ed. *School of the Citizen Soldier: Adapted from the Educational Program of the Second Army*. New York: Appleton-Century, 1942. 558p

Less a personal narrative and more a defense primer providing wide-ranging information, from an explanation of the events that brought the United States into war—making clear the principles for which America fights—to a review of the nation's supply of raw materials and foods vital to the prosecution of the war.

NR 10/19/42, p506. 1200w

NYT 9/20/42, p10. 700w

Groth, John. *Studio: Europe*. New York: Vanguard, 1945. Introduction by Ernest Hemingway. 282p

The author's European odyssey in sketches and text from D-Day to Berlin. In his introduction, Hemingway emphasizes the value of Groth's pictures, most of which capitalize on the artist's fine characterizations and the feeling of action, providing a succinct impression of war's effect on the anonymous people, soldiers, and civilians alike, with its destructiveness to places and things. One reviewer wrote, further: "A few of the best anecdotes concern animals, a mother donkey under shellfire, the rabbit hiding in a church, and a preposterous cow whose carcass we see incredibly pendant in a tree. But the volume is especially a tribute to and a portrait of the soldier, of all sorts of soldiers, shown with candor and respect as they really are."

WBR 11/18/45, p2. 700w

Gunnison, Royal. *So Sorry, No Peace*. New York: Viking, 1944. 272p

Political analysis accompanies Gunnison's story of long months interned as a civilian in a Japanese prison camp, "a home, according to camp authorities, that 'must be loved and cherished.'" Gunnison and his wife, along with thousands of other Americans, suffered many indignities and much nastiness of life under guard before being released for return to the United States on the *Gripsholm* in 1943. Chapters on the Japanese personality derived from daily direct contact with camp officials are hard-hitting.

Nation 11/18/44, p622. 450w

WBR 10/8/44, p5. 1150w

Gunther, John. *D-Day*. New York: Harper, 1944. 276p

Diary record of the Allied landing in Sicily and a trip to the Near East in the summer of 1943. The minuses: too much name-dropping; too much reminiscing about bars and drinking buddies. The pluses: details of the mechanics of a war correspondent's job—writing copy and filing stories that would pass censorship; a memorable portrait of General Eisenhower and the unsettling observation that "the worst thing about war is that so many men like it."

SRL 3/11/44, p11. 1000w

WBR 3/12/44, p3. 1500w

Guttormson, Olga. *Ships Will Sail Again*. Minneapolis, Minn.: Augsburg Publishing House, 1942. 96p

A medical missionary sailing for Africa had her ship sunk by a German Raider, which took aboard some floating survivors. Guttormson relates the story of her many months in prison, later as a relatively free alien living for seven months in Berlin while awaiting

repatriation. The parts of the book which deal with life in the war-
beset capital—replete with air raids, food shortages, boys in Nazi
uniforms, Gestapo agents, wounded German soldiers, dispirited civilians, persecuted Jews ("Jews and dogs verboten") are among the
more unforgettable scenes described by this eyewitness.

Hager, Alice. *Wings for the Dragon: The Air War in Asia.* New York:
Dodd, 1943. 407p

A firsthand account by one of the few women correspondents covering the war, this time in the Burma-China-India theater of operation
where pilots and ground crews never had enough in order to do the
job. When it came to writing about the hard-pressed men who did
the flying and the fighting, the author let the airmen themselves tell
their stories. In addition, Hager exposes the handicaps of bureau-
cratic fumbling, as well as corruption in the higher echelons of the
Chinese government. In passing she mentions the tourist spectacles
enjoyed by the servicemen between their dangerous missions, filled
with the nightlife in Bombay, the fakirs, the Taj Mahal, and other
romantic sights.

    BW 10/28/45, p12. 310w

Haggerty, James. *Guerrilla Padre in Mindanao.* New York: Longmans, 1946. 257p

Personal reminiscences of an American Catholic priest who chose
to stay on in the Philippines after the fall of Bataan. Along with
providing the spiritual needs of his congregation, he acted clandes-
tinely as coordinator, signalman, commissary agent, and otherwise
on behalf of the guerrilla forces operating on Mindanao doing whatever they could to disrupt and impede the efforts of the Japanese invaders.

    NYT 3/10/46, p7. 650w
    WBR 3/10/46, p37. 800w

Hahn, Emily. *Hong Kong Holiday.* Garden City, N.Y.: Doubleday,
1946. 305p

A miscellany of character sketches and impressions about life in the
conquered and beleagued city of Hong Kong, dominated by the victorious Japanese. The final sketch tells of life aboard the Swedish
liner *Gripsholm*, whose mission was to bring refugees safely home
from the war zones.

    NYT 6/23/46, p5. 650w
    WBR 6/23/46, p3. 550w

Hamilton, Esther. *Ambassador in Bonds!* East Stroudsburg, Pa.: Pine-
brook Book Club, 1944.

Missionary writes about her internment experience, including a
good many anecdotes about the Japanese guards and soldiers. "Just

getting enough to eat—Menu: rice, rice soup, fried rice—keeping clean, mending, and doing whatever work for which they were held responsible, took up most of their time." Free moments were used in reading, even studying the Japanese language, or talking to friends in other parts of the camp.

Hammond, Ralph. *My GI Aching Back*. New York: Hobson, 1946.
All about pub-crawling first days in London during the war and the coming invasion, followed by Paris days, ending with reports involving subsequent fighting, including the Battle of the Bulge counteroffensive by the Germans and the eventual Nazi defeat.

Handleman, Howard. *Bridge to Victory: The Story of the Reconquest of the Aleutians*. New York: Random House, 1943. 275p
An eyewitness account of the trials and tribulations of life in the army on the Aleutian front. The long and difficult campaign against the Japanese for control of Attu is reported by correspondent Handleman in considerable detail and is, along with its study of the enemy, a valuable historical record of the war and the people who fought it in that part of the world.
SRL 11/6/43, p5. 1350w
WBR 10/31/43, p1. 2000w

Hannah, Richard. *Tarawa: The Toughest Battle in Marine Corps History*. New York: U.S. Camera, 1944. 126p
An account of the author's experience with the 101st Infantry of the 28th Division and the incredibly hard fighting by Marines over three short days.

Hardin, James. *New York to Oberplan*. Nashville, Tenn.: Mcquiddy Press, 1946.
Author had served with the British Second, the Canadian First, and the American Third armies through campaigns of Normandy, Northern France, the Ardennes, the Rhineland, and Central Europe. Interesting notes on General Patton and an anecdote about Goering's ivory-handled pistol.

Hardison, Priscilla. *The Suzy Q*. Boston: Houghton, 1943. 170p
Secondhand report from a wife's point of view of the problems besetting her husband, the commander of a bomber team, flying the *Suzy Q.*, a "fortress" in action over many parts of the South Pacific. Based on stories of the men who made up the crew, Hardison defines the strained emotions of the airmen at war and the concomitant emotions of the women who await their return.
NYT 12/12/43, p22. 480w
WBR 12/5/43, p2. 600w

Harman, Phillip. *Hellions of Hirohito*. De Vorse, 1944. 213p

This is a factual story of a young American civilian imprisoned and tortured by the Japanese when they conquered Hong Kong. In a foreword by General Russell Hern, who was instrumental in organizing the quasi-military Flying Tigers, there is an interesting personal reaction to the events described in the book in which he states for the record that "I believe there is no race of people on this earth quite as treacherous as the Japanese. Theirs is a treachery veiled by soft words and cunning smiles." Harman's account mostly mirrors this sentiment. The book itself dwells on the inadequacy of the Allied defense in Hong Kong, the brave efforts of the volunteers and civilians to hold the city, and the brutal acts committed by the victorious enemy against British and American civilians. Harman found himself stranded when the city fell, having worked for several years in the East on behalf of the United China Relief agency. Reporting on the beatings, the inadequate food, even the wanton incidents of Japanese soldiers raping women, he tells a story told before, including bouts of dysentery and afflictions of beri-beri while in captivity. Eventually, Harman describes his return to safety in America when he was exchanged for a Japanese national stranded in the United States.

Harmon, Tom. *Pilots Also Pray*. New York: Crowell, 1944. 181p

Autobiography of the former University of Michigan all-American football hero who became an air force pilot. Twice after plane crashes on missions during the war—once in a South American jungle, the second over China—he made his way back to civilization. A devout Catholic, Harmon credited his survival in both cases to his absolute faith in Jesus Christ and, in particular, the Virgin Mary, whose name he invoked many times while lost to help him in his hour of need. Aside from a constant reference to the power of faith to win the day, he expresses a nearly equal confidence in the effectiveness of the planes he flew.

> *Boston Globe* 11/8/44, p19. 440w
>
> *NYT* 11/19/44, p16. 480w

Harrison, Walter. *Log of the Forty-Fifth*. Oklahoma City, Okla., 1941. 81p

A record of service from August 5, 1940, to November 20, 1941, of the splendid outfit of officers and men from Oklahoma, Colorado, New Mexico, and Arizona, training hard, always with the uneasy feeling that they were moving closer and closer to war.

———. *The War Years*. Oklahoma City, Okla., 1945. 102p

The author in his fifties tells of his army service as a public relations officer, a transport commander, on Pentagon duty, joining a special fact-finding mission to North Africa and Italy, while offering the observation that "the army is people. There are good men and lice. . . . There are good officers and sour ones. There are great GIs and some crumbs and cowards." When he was demobilized, Harrison became infuriated by some of the attitudes of his old friends, depressed to find the "moral degeneration" of his hometown (and elsewhere in Wichita, Omaha, Des Moines, Kansas City) where "gyp rackets flourished."

Hasey, John. *Yankee Fighter: The Story of an American in the Free French Legion.* Boston: Little, 1942. 193p

A story of fighting with the French forces in Africa and Syria after the fall of France, told by the *Boston Globe* reporter Joseph Dineen. Along with vivid descriptions of battles in which Hasey took part (and was wounded), there is some preliminary information about time Hasey spent with an ambulance unit serving in Finland.

> *Books* 8/9/42, p5. 1050w
> *NYT* 8/16/42, p8. 1000w

Haskell, Ruth. *Helmets and Lipstick.* New York: Putnam, 1944. 207p

An American army nurse tells of her wartime odyssey which carried her from the United States to Scotland, then England and North Africa, where she cared for the sick and wounded. Haskell herself was hurt during the Libyan campaign, only to be sent to the United States for treatment and, when recovered, was ready to return to the battlefronts.

> *SRL* 4/15/44, p689. 340w

Haugland, Vern. *Vern Haugland's Diary.* Associated Press Pamphlet, 1942. 23p (Also published as *43 Days*, Missoula: Montana State University Press, 1942. 19p)

When a military plane in which Haugland was a correspondent passenger on a flight from Australia to New Guinea encountered bad weather and ran out of fuel over mountains, Haugland parachuted with others of the flight crew into an uninhabited region of southeast New Guinea. "Forty-three days in the jungles of New Guinea . . . without food, under the unceasing tropic rains, forty-three days in the wilderness, with only faith for a guide." But each day a few moments to carefully, painfully scrawl some notes, doing his job as a reporter, struggling wearily through the mud. Accompanied for a while by an officer of the crew until they became separated, later alone, without food for many days (surviving mostly on wild berries) and drenched by frequent heavy rains, the author struggled through nearly impenetrable jungle many days until he reached a native village near the coast where missionaries cared for him. A more detailed narrative of the experience entitled *Letter from New*

Guinea (Farrar, 1943, 148p) becomes a record of conversion to faith to which Haugland attributed his survival as he wandered for nearly seven weeks through forests and over mountains as a miracle from God.

> *NYT* 6/13/43, p4. 1050w
> *WBR* 6/13/43, p2. 1050w

Haynes, George, and **James William**. *The Eleventh Cavalry from the Roer to the Elbe, 1944–1945.* Nurenberg, 1945. 95p

A pamphlet prepared by the Information Education Office of the U.S. Army that tells the story of the 11th Cavalry's participation in World War II, highlighting and personalizing some of the engagements in which the men of this outfit acquitted themselves so well in battles across Western Europe.

Henderson, Harry, and **Herman Moore**. *War in Our Time: A Comprehensive and Analytical History in Pictures and Text of the First Eleven Battles of World War II, Beginning with the Invasion of Manchuria by the Japanese.* Garden City, N.Y.: Doubleday, 1942. 416p

Reproductions of wartime highlights, collected from newspaper photographs taken by correspondent cameramen, depicting the destruction and the victims caused by bombing raids. Analytical text accompanies these and other devastating pictures of war.

> *Books* 12/13/42, p4. 600w
> *NYT* 12/13/42, p2. 360w

Henri, Raymond, et al. *The Marines on Iwo Jima.* New York: Dial Press, 1945. 294p

Three Marine Corps correspondents and two public relations officers combine to relate with grim factuality the story of the battle for Iwo Jima. Simple straightforward report, with a sad list of the dead and missing and casualties suffered in taking the Japanese stronghold.

> *BW* 10/21/45, p12. 360w
> *NYT* 11/25/45, p27. 500w

Herman, Fred. *Dynamite Cargo: Convoy to Russia.* New York: Vanguard, 1943. 158p. Introduction by the popular 1930s movie personality Madeleine Carroll.

One of the early books by a civilian sailor conveying the dangers to which merchant seamen exposed themselves by delivering materials of war to beleaguered Allies. Tells of many harrowing days as part of a convoy hounded by German bombers and submarines. A testimony to contributions and sacrifices in lives lost by men of the merchant service for the war effort.

> *Nation* 5/15/43, p170. 600w
> *WBR* 4/11/43, p5. 750w

Hersey, Harold, ed. *G.I. Laughs: Real Army Humor.* New York: Sheridan, 1944. 255p

Rowdy prose and bawdy drawings (some 200 of them) reflecting the lighter side of military life, selected from jokes and cartoons made by the men in uniform.

Springfield Republican 1/9/44, p7. 300w

WBR 3/12/44, p12. 190w

Hersey, John. *Into the Valley: A Skirmish of the Marines.* New York: Knopf, 1943. 138p

In an article, "Battle of the River," from which *Into the Valley* was expanded, Hersey wrote how "the third battle of the Mataniku River on Guadalcanal was a laboratory sample of thousand of skirmishes our boys are going to have to fight before the war is won. In terms of Stalingrad, or Changsha or El Alemin, it was not a great clash. But it affords an example of how battle feels to men everywhere." Repeating the same message of universality in *Into the Valley*, he said that "the terrain, the weapons and the races of war vary, but certainly never the sensations, except in degree, for they are as universal as those of love." Sharing the dangers of men who had walked into a dense jungle trap, Hersey studied their reaction to battle, to their enemies, and to war in general. The skirmish in which Hersey played an active roll afforded him directly—and the reader vicariously—a glimpse of American young men caught in the grip of ghastly adversity.

NYT 2/7/43, p4. 1000w

Time 2/8/43, p91. 650w

Hesburgh, Theodore. *Letters to Several Women.* Washington, D.C., 1943. 40p

A Catholic priest's letters to women he had known who were now Wacs, Waves, and Lady Marines. In them he discusses a variety of matters centering mostly on exercising care in their behavior, their language, their friends, the places they go, and the kind of recreation they seek, basically to avoid "occasions of sin."

Hill, Helen, and **Violet Maxwell**. *The Children's Garden: The Story of a War-Time Nursery in France.* New York: Macmillan, 1942. 162p

Two women collaborate to tell the true story of a nursery school in wartime France. Hill and Maxwell write how they supervised the children in their care with enterprise and devotion. While the primary appeal of the narrative is to boys and girls under 10 years old, it can also be said to have some historical value.

NYT 12/28/41, p9. 40w

Hill, Justina. *Silent Enemies: The Story of Diseases of War and Their Control*. New York: Putnam, 1942. 266p

By the distinguished bacteriologist author of *Germs and the Man*, the book discusses diseases intensified by war, especially those causing serious infections to the fighting men. Most of the book describes the "new" diseases, which are indigenous to the wartime jungles of the South Pacific and cause debilitating effects. In addition, Hill outlines the efforts of ongoing laboratory experiments at home and those of the medical corps on the fighting fronts.

Hill, Max. *Exchange Ship*. New York: Farrar, 1942. 321p

A book by the press bureau chief in Tokyo, who was arrested when war broke, in which he narrates the story of his treatment by the Japanese before being placed on an exchange ship bound for the United States. Hill also summarizes tales by other American passengers aboard of their treatment at the hands of the Japanese. Voyaging home, Hill heard many stories by American and British citizens about being starved and beaten by Japanese guards, or witnessing others who had been maimed or killed by enemy soldiers in Occupied China. With few exceptions, the Japanese guards were described as cruel and sadistic. Even in earlier peacetime days in Japan, Hill remembers a country galvanized by hatred for the West.

> *Books* 1/17/32, p1. 1250w

Hill, Russell. *Desert War*. New York: Knopf, 1942. 310p

New York Herald Tribune correspondent describes some critical battles in North Africa in 1940–1941 between the British and Rommel's Afrika Korps, filled with advances and retreats and losses and successes on both sides. The Egyptian war, according to Hill, was being fought for a series of objectives: to protect the Nile delta, the Suez Canal, and the oil fields of Iran and Iraq; to help the Russians; to demonstrate the equality in arms of British soldier and German fighter; to eliminate one front (the "western desert") of a two-front war in the Middle East so British defenses could consolidate; and to control the Mediterranean Sea, enabling convoys to move with less threat. While Hill's report covers only the time up until American forces landed in Casablanca, he says that America's "Arsenal of Democracy" played a vital role and contributed to the Allied cause by providing weapons and critical supplies.

> *NYT* 8/16/42, p15. 1050w
>
> *SRL* 8/29/42, p12. 700w

———. *Desert Conquest*. New York: Knopf, 1943. 339p

A companion piece to Hill's earlier *Desert War*, being a close-up report on the back-and-forth campaign waged between the British Eighth Army and the Nazi Afrika Korps. Nontechnical account of rival armies in a life-and-death struggle for control of North Africa and what it looked like to men who did the fighting. There is an appropriate recognition of contributions to victory in Tunisia made by the American Second Corps.

> *NYT* 11/21/43, p47. 280w
>
> *WBR* 10/2/32, p4. 900w

Hind, Robert. *Spirits Unbroken: The Story of Three Years in a Civilian Internment Camp, under the Japanese, at Baguio and at Old Bilibid Prison in the Philippines from December 1941 to February 1945.* San Francisco: Howell, 1945. 291p

The story of three years in enemy internment camps for civilians caught when Japanese invaders took the Philippines. Tells how a group of nonmilitary individuals endured life as war prisoners from December 1941 to February 1945.

> *Christian Science Monitor* 12/4/45, p15. 300w
>
> *WBR* 9/8/47, p16. 600w

Hope, Bob. *I Never Left Home.* New York: Simon & Schuster, 1944. 99p

The American comedy star of radio and movies describes the gags and routines he used to entertain the troops during an 80,000-mile odyssey to far-flung outposts and battlefields, also offering a moving account of how the homesick G.I. overseas endured inimical conditions and hard experiences yet kept on fighting and winning a war.

> *NYT* 6/18/44, p4. 550w
>
> *SRL* 8/19/44, p22. 750w

Hopkins, John. *Diary of World Events: A Chronological Record of the Second World War as Reported Day by Day in American and Foreign Newspaper Dispatches.* Baltimore, Md.: National Advertising, 1943.

The reviews list in *Books*, 1/17/43, sums up the voluminous nature of this work, ultimately valuable for historians dealing with the important events concerning the prelude to war and the war itself. The ten volumes contain 11,000 news clippings in some 2,500 pages, covering the period from Munich through May 1941, the chief sources being the *New York Herald Tribune* and the *Baltimore Sun.*

Horan, James. *Action Tonight: The Story of the Destroyeer* O'Bannon *in the Pacific.* New York: Putnam, 1945. 171p

On the basis of many interviews with those who served on U.S. Destroyer *O'Bannon*, as well as information gathered from official battle reports, Horan has spun what can fairly be called a "yarn," a quasi-realistic story that has an artificial ring to it. Misgivings are in order concerning the reportorial accuracy of the narrative.

> *WBR* 6/24/45, p3. 1200w

Horan, James, and **Gerold Frank**. *Out in the Boondocks: Marines in Action in the Pacific; 21 U.S. Marines Tell Their Stories*. New York: Putnam, 1943. 209p

Twenty-one wounded men from their hospital beds reenact for Horan and Frank how war "would look . . . if you were a Marine," telling of living conditions on the beaches and in the jungles where they fought, offering an insider's view of foxholes, food, snipers, mosquitoes, boondocks, shrapnel, their injuries, and their pain. One sensitive 21-year-old said, "I don't suppose I shall ever be able to sum up the bravery, the guts, the genuine, honest courage displayed by the boys out in Guadalcanal. They were afraid, and yet they took it. They had what it takes."

Nation 9/28/43, p329. 330w

NYT 9/12/32, p7. 800w

Hornsby, Henry, Jr. *The Trey of Sevens*. Dallas: Mathis, 1946. 126p

After training and a few weeks' stay in England, the 777th Field Artillery Battalion, essentially made up of African American soldiers, went to France as part of the Allied drive toward Germany. There is a threefold focus to this book involving the battalion's role in the offensive, episodes of friendly contacts with civilians in Holland and Belgium, and interspersed with comments by Hornsby on the anomaly faced by black soldiers fighting for a country whose principles of equal justice did not yet include them. "We thought about conditions as they exist in the States. We were slated to go into battle soon, and perhaps die for principles that we, as Negroes, had never known. And the heart-rending part about it was that the people we were to fight could get better opportunities in our own country than we could. All they would have to do would be to get there," Hornsby wrote. Again, the author wondered, "Would the ends brought about by the American caste system end with the war, would they continue? . . . We felt that we had the right to defend the United States. It was our homeland. All of our interests and everything that we held dear was a part of it. If the country perished, we too should perish. If the country held, then there was some ray of hope."

Hough, Donald, and **Elliott Arnold**. *Big Distance*. New York: Duell, 1945. 255p

A book that speaks to the debt America owed to the men who flew combat sorties throughout the vast Pacific war zones, narrating the story of the army's air force buildup after Pearl Harbor and describing particular exploits of individual fliers as well as those of one outfit, the 49th Fighter Group.

NYT 10/20/46, p18. 500w

SRL 11/9/46, p18. 650w

———. *Darling, I Am Home*. New York: Norton, 1946. 176p

In the guise of an open letter addressed to his wife, Hough recounts his experience in World Wars I and II for others to read, speaking plainly about foreign (including atom bombs) and domestic (including baseball) affairs and wondering about the value of victories to America and to the rest of the world.

> *NYT* 10/20/46, p18. 500w
>
> *SRL* 11/9/46, p18. 650w

Howard, Fred, and **Janet Howard**. *Whistle While You Wait*. New York: Duell, 1945. 188p

Letters written by an American air force bombardier to his wife, with a few letters written by his wife to him, each recognizing the worthiness of the fight for a better world in the future yet feeling the worry and loneliness of separation in the present.

> *BW* 4/22/45, p3. 300w
>
> *WBR* 4/12/45, p5. 700w

Hubler, Richard, and **John Dechant**. *Flying Leathernecks*. Garden City, N.Y.: Doubleday, 1944. 225p

Account of combat against the enemy by Marine fliers from the early battle at Wake Island over the next three years in the Pacific to the raids on New Britain in 1944, written by two Marine Corps captains. The first part of the book describes the many campaigns against the Japanese fighters and bombers; the second is a collection of word portraits of the men (aces Joe Foss, "Pappy" Boyington, and others) who fought these aerial battles.

> *NYT* 12/10/44, p20. 500w
>
> *WBR* 12/24/44, p7. 350w

Huie, William Bradford. *Can Do! The Story of the Seabees*. New York: Dutton, 1944. 250p

Huie tells the story of the Navy's Construction Battalion (Seabees) and their achievements in the Aleutians, the South Sea Islands, Europe, and North Africa, including a historical survey of the organization, stories of letters sent home, poems written by some of the Seabees, awards earned, and casualties suffered, along with photographs showing Seabees building roads, airfields, living quarters, and docks. Completely dedicated to the proposition that the Seabees are "the goddamndest, toughest and . . . most efficient bunch of hairy-chested broncos who went to war under the stars and stripes," Huie challenged the other branches of the service—navy, army, air force, Marines—to acknowledge the significant contributions made by the Seabees to an American victory. "Our war machine has so many parts, there are so many specialized organizations within organizations, that we shall need to hear each part extolled before we can comprehend the whole."

NYT 9/24/44, p6. 700w

WBR 10/1/44, p5. 800w

————. *From Omaha to Okinawa.* New York: Dutton, 1945. 257p
A companion collection of anecdotes and stories about the Seabees by Huie, who served with the battalion as both an enlisted man and an officer, once again describing the work they did and whatever recreation they could find during the battles of Normandy and Okinawa.

BW 12/23/45, p3. 360w

WBR 12/23/45, p6. 500w

Hunt, George. *Coral Comes High.* New York: Harper, 1946. 1470p
The story of a two-day battle on the island of Peleliu during which only 73 Marines survived out of a rifle company of 235 commanded by the author. Narrative replicates similar experiences suffered by Marines and G.I.s wading ashore against mortar and machine-gun barrages to fight waiting Japanese defenders.

SRL 4/20/46, p46. 550w

WBR 5/5/46, p3. 500w

Huot, Louis. *Guns for Tito.* New York: Fischer, 1945. 273p
Gunrunning exploits of two American officers charged with the assignment of getting weapons and supplies to Marshall Tito in Yugoslavia. Delayed by censors, this published account takes on a slightly fictional gloss as it narrates the details of getting the "guns to Tito" by circumventing the usual regulations and procedures and all the red-tape impediments.

NYT 3/24/44, p6. 500w

WBR 3/18/45, p6. 1100w

Ind, Allison. *Bataan: The Judgment Seat.* New York: Macmillan, 1944. 395p
This book offers the most complete documentation of the Philippine campaign to the fall of Bataan. Having been an eyewitness army officer, Ind is blunt in assessing blame for American misfortunes in the Pacific during the early stages of the war, pointing to national overconfidence, under-preparedness, and some criminal neglect. Includes a record of experiences endured by prisoners held in Japanese camps until the MacArthur liberation.

NYT 3/24/44, p6. 500w

WBR 3/19/44, p3. 1110w

Ingersoll, Ralph. *Action on All Fronts.* New York: Harper, 1942. 330p
Ingersoll's journey around the world took him to Hawaii, the Philippines, Malaysia, China, North Africa, and Russia—at the height

of Soviet battles with Nazi invaders—contributing, along the way, an assessment of the events in the war and an understanding of the issues involved.

    NR 4/13/42, p504. 850w

———. *The Battle Is the Pay-Off.* New York: Harcourt, 1943. 217p

Written by the former chief editor of the liberal tabloid *PM*, the book is a primer on how the army works. Based on his experiences as an officer, Ingersoll synthesizes the long months of training, the organization of various army units, the importance and character of supply, and the part that the officer staff plays in readying an attack. Indeed, 90% of the book describes how an army arranges for 10% of its men to fight. In another way, it may be said that 90% of the book is devoted to bringing the reader to the point where 10% of the men are sent into battle. The battle itself—the culmination of many complicated military factors—is reported in a close-up picture of one engagement in North Africa—the battle of El Guettar in Tunisia—one in which Ingersoll himself took part.

    NYT 10/24/43, p1. 2100w
    SRL 10/23/43, p5. 1100w

———. *Top Secret.* New York: Harcourt, 1946. 373p

Story of the preparations that went into planning the invasion of Normandy, remarking on the military politics involved, conflicts of general staff personalities, widespread confusion, and red-tape obstructions that impeded the effort to ensure a successful action, and offering negative impressions of the British complicity in these matters, including the judgment of Montgomery as an overrated general and an unpleasant man.

    BW 4/21/46, p1. 2050w

Ingham, Travis. *Rendezvous by Submarine: The Story of Charles Parsons and the Guerrilla-Soldiers in the Philippines.* Garden City, N.Y.: Doubleday, 1945. 255p

Guerrilla warfare in the Philippines planned and executed under trying conditions with the help of American forces. Ingram tells the story of "Chico" Parsons, an American married to a Filipino girl, who eluded the Japanese conquerors and helped partisans obtain freedom for their country by organizing Filipino jungle fighters into a guerrilla "army" that bedeviled Japanese occupiers and made MacArthur's return to the islands that much easier.

    BW 10/28/45, p14. 600w
    NYT 10/7/45, p10. 550w

Ingraham, Reg. *First Fleet: The Story of the U.S. Coast Guard at War.* Indianapolis: Bobbs, 1944. 310p

Although essentially a straightforward history of the Coast Guard since its founding to the present, the information provided and incidents reported about the "guardians of our shore line" in World War II underscore the many activities that engage their attention day and night.

BW 3/26/44, p8. 270w

WBR 4/16/44, p12. 800w

Inman, Roger. *Rolley Inman, 1902–1944.* Coffeyville, Kan., 1944. 63p

Letters from Rolley Inman, published by a friend, intended to inform Rolley's acquaintances of his achievements in the years preceding his last flight, when he crashed during bad weather in the mountains of Maine. Combined with flight logs, these letters reveal numerous breathtaking and rollicking exploits of a man who ferried many planes from factories to the war zones in England, Africa, and the Near East as a member of the Air Transport Command. In a serious moment he once wrote, "You mentioned no one being in a hurry to save the country. I have seen so much money wasted and mismanagement, it makes me sick. No wonder Hitler is winning the war. . . . The tax payers would die if they knew how much money was being spent . . . bogged down in red tape and inefficiency."

Jenkins, Burris. *Father Meany and the Fighting 69th.* New York: Fell, 1944, 61p

Tribute by Jenkins to Chaplain Meany who went ashore with the troops at Makin Island and was wounded early in the battle, made even more dramatic by a scene described in which a soldier, shocked by the sight of the bleeding chaplain, tries to administer medical aid and is himself killed as he leans over the fallen priest.

Commonweal 6/30/44, p260. 130w

Springfield Republican 5/9/44, p6. 330w

Jensen, Oliver. *Carrier War.* New York: Simon & Schuster, 1945. 172p

Account of action in the Pacific and the valorous deeds performed by the men who participated in many carrier strikes against the Japanese, from the Marcus raid of September 1943 to the campaign aimed at liberating the Philippines in October 1944.

NYT 2/25/45, p7. 1350w

WBR 2/25/45, p3. 900w

Johnson, Stanley. *The Grim Reapers.* New York: Dutton, 1943. 221p

Narrative detailing the combat story of one of the navy's best fighter squadrons—"Grim Reapers"—in sea/air actions against the Japanese. Bombing strikes at Midway and other enemy land bases are chronicled by Johnson, retelling the story that the men told him about the painstaking way navy pilots are trained, as part of the large background of warfare in the Pacific.

> *NYT* 1/9/44, p20. 650w

> *WBR* 12/12/44, p3. 1100w

Joseph, Franklin. *Far East Report.* Boston: Christopher Publishing, 1946.

Story of flights covering 30,000 miles to nearly every American base and outpost in the Pacific Ocean battle zones and those in other areas of the Far East. The purpose of the mission was to organize squadrons composed of mixed equipment for specialized tasks on Hollandia, Morotai, Manila, Leyte, Zamboanga, Peleliu, Guam, Kwajalein, Hawaii, Tarawa, and New Guinea.

Kahn, Ely. *G.I. Jungle: An American in Australia and New Guinea.* New York: Simon & Schuster, 1943. 150p

A narrative by a former editor of the *New Yorker* who tells of his life at an army camp in Australia and later when he was stationed in New Guinea, adding up to a mostly humorous perspective on a soldier's life overseas. More seriously, Kahn wrote of every phase of jungle warfare he had been a witness to, from the never-ending irritation of mosquitoes to eating C-rations in foxholes and tossing hand grenades through slits in enemy bunkers—the whole range of experiences codified often in narratives of this sort, with the cautionary advice: "You can't ever be certain that a Jap who looks dead is. Judging by their ability to impersonate corpses, I'd say that Japs have more than their share of dramatic talent."

> *WBR* 9/5/43, p4. 500w

Kaltenborn, H. V. *Europe Now: A First-hand Report.* New York. Didier, 1945. 187p

A account of a whirlwind trip by the author during the last five weeks of 1944. The book's table of contents reveals the scope of his fact-finding coverage: "North Africa," "Italy's Dilemma," "Rebirth of France," "The Western Front," "Unflinching Britain!" An overall assessment of Kaltenborn's observations includes a warning that pent-up antagonisms will remain after the end of the war.

> *NYT* 4/22/45, p10. 450w

> *SRL* 4/14/45, p12. 650w

Karig, Walter, and **Welbourn Kelley**. *Battle Report.* Council of Books in Wartime, 1944. 499p

Record of naval activities in the Pacific from Pearl Harbor to the Battle of the Coral Sea. Using official reports, eyewitness testimony, and correspondents' dispatches and accounts, the book mixes chronology, history, human-interest vignettes, incidents of courage, resourcefulness, and heroism, humorous moments, and days of devastation compiled about the fleet by two navy officers.

>*BW* 12/10/44, p10. 1400w
>
>*NYT* 12/10/44, p19. 550w

Kelly, Charles. *One Man's War*. New York: Knopf, 1944. 182p

A celebrated war hero from Pittsburgh, Sergeant "Commando" Kelly relates his adventures in battle. The book reveals a young man, part hero and part reckless and carefree American boy, who sums up his Congressional Medal of Honor exploits for extraordinary feats of fighting in this way: "The GI's slice of battle is the most mixed up, confused and bewildering thing. . . . Officers and men pop up for a second or a day, whose names he doesn't know, and he may never see them again. The ground around him shakes or turns into a swamp. A river runs at his feet, and all he knows is . . . that he's been told to cross it." In the process, Kelly admits to knowing many comrades who fought as he did or harder—and many who died who received no recognition or medals for their bravery.

>*WBR* 9/17/44, p19. 550w

Kerwin, Paschal. *Big Men of the Little Navy*. Paterson, N.J.: St. Anthony Guild Press, 1946.

A Catholic priest details the adventures of an amphibious force in the Mediterranean during the campaigns in North Africa, the Salerno landings, and the assaults on the west coast of Italy, as well as the invasion of southern France—the sort of operations which added many words to our everyday language: D-Day, H-Hour, landing barges, half-tracks, amphibs, etc. Kerwin attempts to give the lowdown on what made the amphibious forces click, assigning some credit to the part the Big Men in the Small Navy (landing crafts) played in successful beachhead assaults.

Kirchberg, W., S. F. Kogot, J. J. Cleary, et al. *Our 15 Months Aboard the Henry Lomb*. Place of publication unspecified: Privately printed, 1944. 32p

This is an unusual wartime narrative in its lighthearted report involving the dangerous job of a Liberty class cargo ship's merchant seamen delivering supplies to Allied forces overseas. Aside from rough-weather crossings and occasional minor threats from enemy planes and subs, the focus of the narrative centers around the diverse crew from "over half the states in the union . . . of all ages [and] all walks of life . . . farmers, hack drivers, clerks, musicians, bartenders, bootleggers, horse players, and crap shooters." One episode tells of the ship having become a floating kennel because of all the dogs on board kept by the seamen; another of a party on shore at a Long Island restaurant ("Yes, sir. War was forgotten that night. Who wanted to be bothered with thoughts of submarines, the Scharnhorst, or the Von Tirpitz, or for that matter, ice, snow, fog, and heavy seas in the North Atlantic? We were home, for the time being at least, and singing that well-known favorite of Kate Smith, 'God Bless America,' with renewed sincerity.") A third episode details the musical talents of the "Henry Lomb Corn Cobblers," playing the new songs such as "The Flop-Eared Mule" and "The Twelfth Street Rag," and a description of a Christmas party at sea, celebrated with "a tree, wreaths, ornaments and other festive decorations."

Klemmer, Harvey. *They'll Never Quit*. New York: Funk, 1941. 321p

As a tribute to the indomitable spirit of the British people when German bombers rained terror on their cities, Klemmer provides a comprehensive account of the suffering and deprivation borne in the war-torn little island. "These Englishmen are tough babies," he wrote, "and don't let anyone tell you otherwise." Along with his admiration for how the British coped, the author points to lessons Americans can learn from them.

Books 3/2/41, p2. 650w

NYT 3/9/41, p3. 750w

Klitgaard, Kaj. *Oil and Deep Water*. University of North Carolina Press, 1945. 182p

Account of an experienced seaman, who shipped out on a tanker bound for North Africa with oil for American troops, filled with thoughtful convictions about war and peace and the role the merchant men who sailed cargo ships played in the achievements of both. Besides routine details of work onboard, Klitgaard assumes the role of social critic, remarking on many issues which might challenge the peace when it comes, especially the place of colonial empires in a more enlightened world, concluding with a recognition of democracy in action regarding the achievements of an ethnically diverse crew successfully doing a job together.

BW 10/21/45, p2. 450w

WBR 10/14/45, p14. 1200w

Knox, Frank. (Secretary of the Navy). *Lest We Forget!* Washington, D.C.: Industrial Incentive Division, Navy Department, 1943. 15p

Excerpts from eight wonderful letters "written by men and women of every rank and age, who share alike the Navy's blue and gold and its imperishable traditions. . . . Their [letters] are the more revealing because they were never intended for publication. . . . Reading between these lines we cannot fail to see our debt to these countrymen of ours who lived, and often died, the American way" (preface).

Among the letters is one written by William R. Evans Jr. of Torpedo Squadron Eight to a friend, shortly before he was reported missing in action at the Battle of Midway. Ensign Evans writes of the fearless bravery of American young men "who were never trained for war, and who almost never believed in war, but who have, from some hidden source, brought forth a gallantry which is homespun." Another, from the last letter Commander John J. Shea wrote to his son before he was reported missing in action: "Fighting for the defense of our country's ideals and homes is an honor and a duty which your daddy has to do before he comes home." The remaining six excerpts sound similar notes—boys who "were carrying on like men"; a severely wounded sailor "with his abdomen blown to bits . . . begged the doctor to save one of those other fellows who still has a fighting chance."

Landis, Carole. *Four Jills in a Jeep*. New York: Random House, 1944. 182p

Four prominent Hollywood actresses bring fun and reminders of home to troops stationed in England and North Africa. Martha Raye, Mitzi Mayfair, Kay Francis, and Carole Landis, who wrote this account of their traveling road show, typify the experiences of many USO companies helping to boost the morale of servicemen all over the globe. (*See personal narratives of* Joe E. Brown, Jerry Colonna, Bob Hope, and Alexander Schacht.)

> *NYT* 6/4/44, p29. 400w
> *Theatre Arts* 5/44, p320. 140w

Lardner, John. *Southwest Passage: The Yanks in the Pacific*. Philadelphia: Lippincott, 1943. 302p

An informal, mostly humorous tale by a former sports columnist about his stay in Australia, describing the people, their customs, their speech, and—what Lardner especially came to appreciate—their independent views; in short, everything that American servicemen encountered "Down Under." The book includes a glossary of Australian slang.

> *NYT* 3/21/43, p2. 1050w
> *WBR* 3/21/43, p7. 1050w

Lawson, Ted. *Thirty Seconds over Tokyo*. New York: Random House, 1943. 221p

After the interesting but generally mundane matter of long preparations for a historic mission (a retaliatory air raid by a group of B-17s, destination Tokyo, leaving from the short deck of a U.S. carrier sailing as close to Japan as militarily advisable), the months of simulated practice, the weeks of waiting, the hours of geography lessons, the drama of the exploit suddenly takes shape. When a

Japanese patrol boat was spotted, it required a much earlier bomber liftoff than planned, farther from the target areas, and the need to skim 20 feet above wave crests in order to avoid detection by enemy radar. Finally, Mt. Fujiyama loomed before them, looking like the images remembered from the Japanese stamps collected in childhood. In the end, the Doolittle mission lost every plane, 11 airmen were captured or killed, and several seriously wounded. In retrospect, the raid had a shovel of strategic value mixed with a pailful of positive effect on home-front morale.

> *NYT* 7/11/43, p1. 1500w
> *WBR* 7/11/43, p1. 2850w

Lay, Beirne. *I've Had It: The Survival of a Bomber Group Commander.* New York: Harper, 1945. 144p

Colonel Lay had his plane shot down a few weeks before the D-Day invasion at Normandy. He tells how he and his copilot parachuted to safety in enemy-held France, but eluded capture and eventually managed to escape with the help of resistance organizations operating in the French countryside. Colonel Lay's book is not limited to his adventures in escaping. Early chapters describe the "weird sensation . . . taking off on instruments . . . while you guide thirty tons of roaring bomber down an unseen runway . . . like a blind man on a toboggan slide."

> *NYT* 11/25/45, p7. 700w
> *WBR* 1/6/46, p3. 850w

Lea, Tom. *Peleliu Landing.* San Antonio, Tex.: Hertzog, 1945. 34p

"A simple narrative of an experience in battle [the assault on Peleliu in the Pacific] . . . like combat itself . . . personal, confused, benumbed and in its deepest sense lonely," the author, a *Life* artist, remarked at the beginning of his narrative, before telling his story of being with the Marines under fire for the first 32 hours of combat. His purpose: to record the men in action. Not able to do any sketching or writing on the spot, Lea memorized what he saw and felt while trying to stay alive through the enemy attacks. Interspersed with his narrative of the experience are sketches of the invasion—four Marines dead on the hot coral sands, a burning landing craft, assault against a block house, snipers, sick bay in a shell hole, a chaplain reading scriptures.

Lee, Clark. *They Call It Pacific.* New York: Viking, 1943. 374p

Lee, an Associated Press correspondent whose "beat" since pre-Pearl Harbor was such venues as Tokyo and Shanghai, describes what Pacific-region war was like. He was with the beleaguered troops on Bataan, and reported action on Guadalcanal and the fighting around the Solomon Islands. With an occasional personal anecdote, the book is made up of military facts which had been previously censored. Mostly straightforward journalism—with the keynote observation of an air corps sergeant bemoaning the lack of planes and equipment: "Tell them [at home] that this isn't only our war, it's the war of every American."

NYT 3/21/43, p4. 900w

SRL 4/24/43, p11. 1050w

Lest We Forget: The Twenty-Fourth Evacuation Hospital. United States Printing Office, 1943.

This is the story of a hospital unit formed and activated for the purpose of caring for the anticipated battlefield fallen, detailing the training to accomplish its mission, from maneuvers in Tennessee to embarkation in New York, then arrival in England followed by its D-Day assignment in France, including a blow-by-blow account of the role the Twenty-Fourth Evacuation Hospital played in treating the large number of casualties during and after the breakthrough against German defenses in Western Europe, which led to winning the battle of France.

Lesuer, Laurence. *Twelve Months That Changed the World.* New York: Knopf, 1943. 345p

Describes Russian military strength in terms of the reactions and spirit of a people confident of victory, demonstrated by housewives building barricades and digging tank-traps, a woman pilot who commanded an all-male squadron of bombers, patriotic children crippled in defense of their homeland, and, in spite of the many hardships, cheering each other up.

Nation 8/28/43, p246. 1100w

NYT 7/30/44, p6. 440w

Lewis, Warfield, ed. *Fighting Words.* Philadelphia: Lippincott, 1944. 130p

A collection of stories and cartoons, done by members of the Armed Forces, submitted originally to a contest sponsored by the wartime Service League, adding up to a composite portrait of the U.S. fighting man unlike the romantic stereotype of the popularly conveyed image of the wisecracking heroic American.

BW 8/12/44, p6. 310w

NYT 7/30/44, p6. 440w

Liebling, A. J. *Road Back to Paris.* Garden City, N.Y.: Doubleday, 1944. 300p

Comprises the bulk of *New Yorker* essays written by the author about his travels, beginning with Paris shortly after war broke out until French capitulation to the Nazis, later to London and North Africa. Short on military and political developments and long on delineating the sense and moods of the little people who bore the brunt of the fighting.

NYT 1/23/44, p5. 900w

WBR 2/6/44, p5. 110w

Litz, Leo. *Report from the Pacific*. Indianapolis News, 1946.

Story of a war correspondent for the *Indianapolis News* whose assignment was to cover the war in the Pacific, focusing on Hoosiers in service wherever he might find them. Replete with human interest reporting, humorous anecdotes, and character studies gathered as he mingled with sailors, soldiers, airmen, Seabees—from the lowest enlisted personnel to the highest ranking officers, all of them imbued with the spirit that could only result in victory for Allied causes.

Lodge, Henry Cabot, et al. *Report on the War*. United States Government Printing Office, 1943.

Observations by five members of the U.S. Senate based on the results of a fact-finding tour covering 45,000 miles to various war fronts. In addition to Lodge, senators Richard Russell, Albert Chandler, Ralph Brewster, and James Mead made the trip and contributed to the report.

Long, Frances. *Half a World Away: From Boarding School to Jap Prison*. New York: Farrar & Rinehart, 1943. 243p

An account by the daughter of a consular official about her wartime captivity after Manila surrendered to Japanese forces. Long writes of her arrest and her experiences at Santo Tomas, a Philippines detention camp, until finally being put on an exchange ship bound for the United States.

NYT 8/29/43, p4. 280w

WBR 8/22/43, p12. 650w

Look, *My Favorite War Story*; compiled by the editors of *Look*, 1945. 241p

Thirty-four war correspondents, many known from their newspaper dispatches and radio talks, contributed abridged (no more than 1,000 words) tales of their most memorable war experiences, in which every theater of operation and every possible mood are represented.

BW 10/20/45, p2. 70w

WBR 11/18/45, p24. 130w

Lowell, Juliet. *Dear Sir*. New York: Duell, 1944. 75p

A collection of letters taken from the files of draft boards, the OPA, war plant offices, and various government agencies, humorously unveiling the problems and perplexities of American citizens in wartime. Following are excerpts from sample letters sent to various

Selective Service offices: "Gentlemen: I think I shud be placed in 4F since my doktor says I have an ulcer in my large intestical." "Shud I apply for draft exemption? I'm a homosexual but in time expect to become a bisexual." "Gentlemen: I want to inform you that my status has changed. My wife gave birth to a baby and I want to thank every member of the local board." "Gentlemen: I believe in being honest with you because you'd probably find it out sooner or later anyway. Seven months ago you classified me 3A as long as I continued to support my Father. Well, I don't support him any longer. Yesterday he was drafted." In addition to letters written to rent control boards, the Red Cross, banks, and several war plants are those written by servicemen to their commanding officers like one from Private Leonard K——: "Dear Colonel, After four months of Army life and much sober reflection, I have decided that I cannot support my wife in the manner to which she has become accustomed on my Army pay of $50 a month. Kindly consider this my resignation from the Armed forces. Private Leonard K——."

    BW 7/23/44, p2. 250w

Lucas, Jim. *Combat Correspondent*. New York: Reynal, 1944. 210p

Except for a disturbing account of the bloody fighting at Tarawa, the narrative by this Marine who carried a typewriter along with a rifle tells a generally pleasant story of his many experiences with the men in boot camp, on assault beaches, in foxholes, through jungles, on bombing raids, even a submarine mission.

    NYT 9/17/33, p3. 440w

    WBR 9/24/44, p5. 1150w

Lutz, Alma. *With Love, Jane*. New York: Day, 1945. 199p

This is a collection of letters written by women in the military, many of them from war fronts. Some excerpts from letters come from those who spent time in muddy foxholes, or were sickened at the sight of bats and rats in the jungles of New Guinea, revealing the new and terrible experiences many of them endured. One army nurse wrote, "The other nations are real and exist and have to be treated as groups of people with the same rights and wants as Americans and there's no wanting to protect ourselves first and at the expense of others." A Wac sergeant wrote, "Democracy and the American way of life improve by comparison with others, although many of us are realizing how provincial we are as a people." Another army nurse described the grim slaughter of war, remarking that "at the height of battle the ambulances start rolling in until the overflow has to lie on litters outside the receiving tent." Another Wac wrote, "There is no advantage in war except what the individual makes for himself. In the Army we lose eccentricities, prejudices, pettiness, because they cannot survive in the face of matter-of-fact and non-luxurious living." In their small way, these letters are valuable documents which help to write the history of World War II.

NYT 11/18/45, p18. 600w

Lyne, Mary, and **Kay Arthur**. *Three Years Behind the Mast: The Story of the United States Coast Guard SPARS*. The Coast Guard Information Center Publication, 1946. 126p

An introductory note explains how, at a time when manpower was critically short, women joined the service in increasing numbers, and the Coast Guard SPARS became an option. Women replaced the men who went to sea and carried the fight to the enemy. SPARS had a job to do and went to work with enthusiasm, efficiency, and a minimum of fanfare. This narrative tells of boot training and barracks life, the routine jobs, and the military hazards of "as Salty, Shipshape and Gallant a Crew as Never Sailed the Seven Seas," and "the fun, the hard work, the dreariness of association, the despairs and frustrations, the immense pride in being a small part of the Coast Guard."

Lynip, Louise. *On Good Ground*. Erdmans, 1946. 149p

This is a collection of missionary stories from the Philippines during the Japanese occupation. Along with others, Lynip made her "way farther into the hills and [was] successful in hiding out from the Japanese for over two years, learning lessons of faith, trust, and complete dependence upon their Lord. . . . The stories in this book are true accounts of some of the many experiences with the mountain folk of Bukidnon . . . the reader will find a demonstration of practical Christianity in a primitive setting, showing . . . how a missionary finds opportunities to show love, compassion, and power of Christ just by being faithful from day to day" (foreword). "These are true stories of the Lord's dealing with the people of Bukidnon, told as the author heard them or as they were observed" (preface). There is the story of Marcella, "child of the forest," who accepted Christianity then lost it when a child of hers died of pneumonia, but when a second daughter came, her faith was restored. From the chapter "Josefa: Upon Whom the Light Shined" to "Linda: A Little Child Shall Lead Them" and "Susanna: Hand Maiden of the Lord," the theme is the same: belief in Jesus Christ would console a hungry body and a weary spirit. This was the missionary's purpose in the Philippines—to convert those who had not been exposed to the awesome healing power of Christianity. "Then suddenly one morning everything changed. War was declared! The island was invaded. Homes along the road must be abandoned. The American missionaries, cut off from their own country, were stranded—their lives at the mercy of a people who wavered uncertainly under the impact of the enemy's force. Until this day the missionary's home had offered the greatest security to the children who had found refuge there. Now it was stripped of its security. An American's home was the most dangerous place in which to be."

MacKay, Helen. *With Love for France.* New York: Scribner, 1942. 139p

Verbal portraits of France, French life, and the people—between the start of war in September 1939 and the beginning of the German occupation of the country in June 1940—written by a devoted Francophile. This is a book of days and scenes and episodes about men, women, and children of a France that had become once again "the world's battlefield." When the Germans made Paris theirs, "everything was quite over, our hope and our belief." Nonetheless, MacKay worked for a time among the poor and uprooted refugees of war.

NYT 5/24/42, p6. 900w

MacKenzie, Colin. *Sailors of Fortune.* New York: Dutton, 1944. 190p

Narrative of an American merchant seaman possessed neither of any special patriotism nor high ideals, who rarely exhibited any dislike for the enemy or any understanding of what the fighting was all about, but nevertheless sailed on a tanker across the Atlantic infested with marauding German submarines. He wrote his book "to show these [merchant sailors] to you and perhaps you'll begin to see what kind of men we are who go to sea with the stuff of war and who endure hardships most people would die from, or go crazy from, or both." MacKenzie's ship was torpedoed twice; the first explosion broke his leg, the second sank the ship.

WBR 5/282/44, p12. 500w

MacKenzie, DeWitt. *Men Without Guns.* Blakiston, 1946. 47p

Over 100 color reproductions of paintings and sketches done by several artists attached to the medical corps during the war, dramatizing, with descriptive text, the work of the medical corps in frontline, first-aid stations and larger medical hospitals in the rear. Among other scenes, the book depicts the compelling urgency of doctors and nurses caring for boys unlucky enough to have been wounded or performing the grim task of wrapping stiff bodies of those less fortunate in sheets and shrouds.

Atlantic 4/46, p154. 800w
WBR 2/10/46, p6. 850w

MacVane, John. *Journey into War: War and Diplomacy in North Africa*. New York: Appleton-Century, 1943. 330p

An NBC correspondent's report on the Anglo-American offensive along the rim of Africa, including focus on the American thrust from El Guettar and the British battle at Mareth, interspersed with noteworthy comments on the machinations involved in dealing with the Vichy government installed in Algeria.

NR 1/31/44, p157. 800w

SRL 12/11/43, p32. 700w

Madden, Paul. *Survivor*. Bruce, 1944. 68p

The story of Paul Madden, who survived the ordeal of being adrift for 11 days with two other fliers, when his plane ditched in the Atlantic for lack of fuel. On a raft stocked with food, water, fishing tackle, compass, even a small sail, floating in an area heavily patrolled by planes and ships, the men assumed that rescue would be a matter of time. Days passed, however, and no rescue came. More than that, the raft kept capsizing in heavy ocean swells, causing the loss of most of their food, drinking water, and equipment. Thereafter, it meant the steady weakening of all three through the exertion of righting the raft and climbing aboard time and again. Captain Hart swallowed a great quantity of saltwater and died on the sixth day. Private Elsie died the 11th day, slipping away and sinking after another capsizing. Only Madden survived. As in other "survivor" tales (*see* Rickenbacker, Harmon), there is a religious interpretation sounded by an author as the only one who lived through the ordeal.

NYT 9/10/44, p6. 440w

Maguire, William. *The Captain Wears a Cross*. New York: Macmillan, 1943. 207p

A navy chaplain "tells of Catholic, Protestant and Jews, of serene men and worried men; of heroic death in the line of duty and of long lives devoted to that same duty" (foreword). The impression given in the book is that the preponderance of chaplaincy in the navy was almost universally a Catholic affair, an impression belied by the fact that there were many chaplains serving in all the military branches, and on the front lines with the fighting men who were Protestants and Jews.

Maisel, Albert. *The Wounded Get Back*. New York: Harcourt, 1944. 230p

An account of the successful application of medicine and surgery to the particular needs of modern warfare, delivered to the wounded on fully equipped hospital ships and large base hospitals. Lacing his study with occupational jargon and technical detail—but not so much that a layperson would be lost—Maisel authenticated the proficiency of U.S. Navy medics and surgeons, assuring friends and family that nothing had been neglected and no expense had been spared to make certain that wounded loved ones *do get back* in order to resume their normal peacetime lives.

>   *NYT* 5/21/44, p5. 700w

>   *WBR* 5/21/44, p6. 850w

Maloney, John. *Let There Be Mercy: The Odyssey of a Red Cross Man.* Garden City, N.Y.: Doubleday, 1941. 337p

A record of one man's travels through 15 countries from the Arctic through Scandinavia, the low countries, France, Spain, and North Africa, prompting him "to give American readers some idea of the unspeakable hardships and suffering that the little people of Europe—the peasants, the shopkeepers and their clerks, the doctors and lawyers, the fathers and mothers, the children too young to understand the turmoil breaking around them—were forced to endure through the first eighteen months of Hitler's war" (author's note). Everywhere, in addition to consulting with officials, Maloney recorded the words of soldiers, refugees, and others caught in the maelstrom of war in order to buttress a lecture concerning "human hate . . . and mass slaughter for those at home who have no idea of what war is" (foreword).

>   *NYT* 11/9/41, p15. 850w

>   *SRL* 12/6/41, p24. 600w

Maloney, Tom. *U.S.A. at War.* New York: Duell, 1944. 304p

A visual documentary showing the panorama of fighting on all the world's battlefronts, from the jungles of New Guinea to the rubble of Cassino, evoking the roar of bombers and the chaos of invasion, certifying the endurance and courage of Americans at war.

>   *NYT* 12/17/44, p7. 900w

>   *WBR* 12/10/44, p2. 650w

Marsdan, Lawrence. *Attack Transport.* University of Minnesota Press, 1946. 200p; 26 black-and-white photographs

Marsdan tells the story of the attack transports that "carry the bulk of the troops and equipment to the bloody assault . . . landings. . . . These ships arrive with the initial amphibian attacks and continue their support throughout the fighting. Unarmored and with small fire power, they yet carry a great weapon that is war's one essential combat element: the troops that fight on the ground" (foreword). The story is told by Marsdan in the first person, from the time the ship was commissioned, describing the war in the Pacific from the point of view of one small ship, the USS *Doyen*, and the day-to-day life of the men who sailed her. While it's the story of one ship, it is representative of many ships like it and the personnel of those other attack transports. The assaults on Tarawa, Leyte, Iwo Jima, among others, are recounted.

>   *Books* 8/9/42, p1. 1700w
>   *NYT* 8/9/42, p3. 1150w

Martin, Ralph. *Boy from Nebraska.* New York: Harper, 1946. 208p

A message narrative about Ben Kuroki, a Japanese American boy from Nebraska, who had never known bigotry at home yet in the army he encountered it often. In this way, Kuroki's story of his experiences is the story of many Japanese Americans who courageously fought in other regiments of the U.S. Army, which by extension, as Bill Mauldin points out in his introduction, were duplicated in the lives of millions of African Americans who were willing to fight and sometimes die in a war against racist enemies, even though they had suffered widespread racial prejudice at home.

>   *NYT* 11/3/46, p18. 450w
>   *SRL* 11/9/46, p18. 600w

Mauldin, Bill. *Up Front.* New York: World, 1945. 228p

An intimate look into a soldier's battlefield life through a collection of cartoons featuring the picaresque characters of foot-slogging Willy and Joe, representative infantrymen who share a foxhole and a rubbled building. With interpretative text, the material touches on soul-searching evocations of terror covered over by a sustaining sardonic humor and bleak loneliness, relieved by two hearts enduring the emptiness together.

>   *NYT* 6/17/45, p1. 2100w
>   *WBR* 6/17/45, p1. 100w

Maule, Henry, ed. *Book of War Letters.* New York: Random House, 1943. 328p

Letters from servicemen and women of all ranks, branches, and backgrounds to home folks in every part of the United States that provide illuminating insights of their feelings about war, friendship, family, while revealing how homesick, sensitive, caring, serious, and funny young Americans were under the most trying conditions. Informative, cogent revelations of moods generated by war, from every place Americans were stationed, whether camps at home, battlefronts overseas, or lonely outposts far from the fighting.

>   *BW* 11/21/43, p3. 450w
>   *NYT* 11/28/43, p3. 1300w

McBride, William, et al. *Anybody Here from Jersey?* Passaic, N.J., 1945. 274p

The collected stories of three *Herald-News* war correspondents— William McBride, Carl Ek, and Rodney Odell—who covered the war from Europe and the South Pacific, but instead of reporting battles wrote stories about officers and enlistees who went to war from 20 communities in the Passaic-Bergen county area. Correspondents report on the small talk and longings for home. Although they encountered Jerseyites only now and again, Odell explained, "there was little to distinguish a New Jersey soldier from a boy of the Los Angeles suburbs. . . . Most of them swore and prayed and drank and repented."

McCoy, Melvyn, and **Stephen Mellnik**. *Ten Escape from Tojo*. New York: Farrar, 1944. 106p

An account of the mistreatment and atrocities suffered by American servicemen at the hands of the Japanese soldiers after the fall of Corregidor. Most of the story describes brutal guards, poor food, unsanitary facilities, and absence of medical care. Two of the prisoners, both American officers, also tell the story of their escape from the internment camp. The authors are reticent about this part of the story in order to protect prisoners left behind and Filipino civilians who might have helped their flight.

    NYT 3/12/44, p1. 500w

    WBR 3/25/44, p4. 750w

McCoy, Samuel. *Nor Death Dismay: A Record of Merchant Ships and Merchant Mariners in World War II*. New York: Macmillan, 1941. 248p

A summary of the contributions made by the men who sailed on cargo ships carrying vital supplies through dangerous submarine-infested waters, including descriptions of lives that merchant sailors led in wartime. Lots of action.

    NYT 7/30/44, p4. 500w

    Springfield Republican 9/24/44, p4. 600w

McCracken, Kenneth. *Baby Flattop*. New York: Farrar, 1944. 108p

Sketches of uneventful experiences connected with duty aboard the USS *Princess*, a small version of the larger carriers *Lexington* and *Saratoga*, with sea life aboard both classes of ships being just about the same. Sketches of how sailors live and work during brief yet violent action (hours), but mostly over long stretches (months) of inaction.

    BW 8/13/44, p6. 320w

    WBR 8/27/44, p10. 350w

McCrary, John, and **Davis Scherman**. *First of the Many*. New York: Simon & Schuster, 1944. 214p

A combination yearbook and journal recounting the exploits of the officers and men of the Army's Eighth Air Corps, beginning with the first time 12 B-17s bombed Rouen in August 1943, to a time when hundreds of Liberators and Flying Fortresses and their companies of brave airmen flew missions to many cities on the Continent, battering German factories and railroads and shore installations in order to make less difficult the eventual D-Day assault on Normandy. By far, the most valuable aspect of the book is the 128 pages of action photographs. Given the generous collection of photographs, along with verbal portraits of the men and boys who were among "the first of many" invaders of Germany (if only from the air), the book shows both the sacrifices made and the profit gained through high-altitude bombing by machines, the products of American ingenuity, and by men, the product of American values.

McKeogh, Michael, and **Richard Lockridge**. *Sgt. Mickey and General Ike.* New York: Putnam, 1946. 185p

A soldier who was Eisenhower's orderly throughout the war offers a warm and generous estimate of the Allied Commander as a great soldier and a great man—"a Clark Gable in . . . uniform."

NYT 8/4/46, p12. 410w

WBR 5/19/46, p28. 750w

McRoberts, Duncan. *While China Bleeds.* Grand Rapids, Mich.: Zondervan Press, 1943. 165p

As part of an evangelical crusade in wartime China, McRoberts tells of the savagery of the Japanese invaders and the intense suffering visited on the people under their domination, only assuaging his distress with the constant reminder of "the message of Calvary [as] mighty and powerful," identifying "the suffering of Jesus Christ with those who now suffer equally."

Mead, James. *Tell the Folks Back Home.* New York: Appleton-Century, 1944. 298p

After a fact-finding journey with four colleagues from the U.S. Senate, Mead wrote the book because he wanted to share as widely as possible "the great experience of this trip around a war-torn world." Among other things, Mead was shocked at seeing the thousands of starving Indians in the streets of Calcutta, weary of the maneuvering already taking place among the French North Africans for postwar advantages, and moved by the number of homesick Americans he encountered everywhere he went. There are also personal anecdotes about Churchill, MacArthur, and other world figures.

BW 5/7/44, p1. 900w

NYT 5/14/44, p3. 650w

Mears, Frederick. *Carrier Combat.* Garden City, N.Y.: Doubleday, 1944. 150p

Yet another flattop narrative, *Carrier Combat* fulfills its description: "A secret approach by sea to within aircraft range of the objective, an undiscovered flight to the target, bombs and torpedoes dropped, installations and transports strafed with . . . heroic and grim determination . . . producing [another] great victory for America." The central episode of the narrative involves what naval historians have criticized as a reckless tactical endeavor—Commander Waldron of the *Hornet* ordering a virtual suicide attack, "which had no hope of success . . . sacrificing men and planes" against the enemy in order to gain a questionable first-blow psychological advantage. While others were "bewildered" by the enormity of American losses—14 of 15 planes in the squadron failed to survive—Mears, before he himself was killed in action, provided his own perspective on the controversy. On the one hand, he offers a standard military rationalization: "In the Navy . . . you do what you are told to do, and if some of your comrades are killed in the process, it's tough to take but it doesn't change anything." Beyond that, while Mears frankly admits the fear he felt when fighting against Zeroes that far outnumbered his squadron or diving into the incredible firepower of Japanese cruisers, he can still offer arguably valid explanations of the many tactical benefits achieved by Waldron's "reckless" boldness, which critics did not "fully understand [concerning] the tactical situation prevailing that . . . black and bitter . . . day." In the end, Mears felt that "the annihilating defeat dealt the enemy had been worth the price many times over."

NYT 1/16/44, p12. 480w

WBR 1/23/44, p23. 250w

Mellor, William. *Sank Same*. New York: Howell-Sorkin, 1944. 244p

Well-documented report of the efforts of the Civilian Air Patrol and Coast Guard Rescue Units constantly cruising along the waters off the American coast, in good weather and bad, on the lookout for German U-boats lying in wait for merchant ships. Manned mostly by overage civilians, they routinely patrolled with only occasional spots of excitement, doing a modest job through many weary months with little recognition or remuneration.

SRL 12/22/44, p15. 700w

WBR 11/26/44, p5. 700w

Mercey, Arch, and **Lee Grove**, eds. *Sea, Surf and Hell: The United States Coast Guard in World War II*. New York: Prentice-Hall, 1945. 352p

Commander Mercey and Chief Specialist Grove collaborated on this "anthology" of brief articles about the activities of the Coast Guard on North Atlantic patrol. Many sailors of the United States Coast Guard contributed stories, which ran the gamut from comedy to tragedy, from courage to cunning, mostly based on experiences of individual crew members and some taken from official logbooks, providing a mix of journalism and adventure. One incident tells of attempts to dislodge Nazis from Greenland; another describes the heroic efforts of coastguardsmen in helping to extinguish a burning ammunition ship in New York Harbor; a third details the hunt for enemy U-boats off the U.S. coast. An appendix includes Coast Guard songs and ditties and there is a glossary of nautical terms.

> *BW* 11/25/45, p3. 360w
>
> *SRL* 9/15/42, p6. 1100w

Michie, Allan. *Retreat to Victory.* Alliance, 1942. 498p

Author takes the odd position that setbacks suffered at Dunkirk, Pearl Harbor, and the Philippines, unpleasant as they were, are all to be seen as contributions to an ultimate victory, reasoning that in every case they deprived the enemies of men, materiel, and time.

> *Books* 9/42, p4. 1350w
>
> *SRL* 9/15/42, p6. 1100w

———. *Air Offensive Against Germany.* New York: Holt, 1943. 151p

Tells what Michie thinks is wrong with the past and present air offensive against Germany, and what he thinks should be done to perfect the future offensive so that victory in the West may be achieved in 1943, advocating night bombing by the American Air Force with special targets of enemy industrial towns.

> *NYT* 2/21/43, p3. 1000w
>
> *NR* 4/5/43, p452. 950w

Michie, Allan, and **Walter Graebner**, eds. *Their Finest Hours: First-hand Narratives of the War in England.* New York: Harcourt, 1941. 226p

Airmen, firefighters, men on a convoy, a Coventry doctor, a girl warden, and many others tell of their personal experience in the war; the human note being sounded in stories such as from the woman who describes the day her house was bombed and another about the sinking of a freighter.

> *New Statesman and Nation* 1/25/41, p88. 900w
>
> *Time* 4/7/41, p98. 400w

Middleton, Drew. *Our Share of Night.* New York: Viking, 1946. 380p

Impressions of six years of war, from the battle of Poland, England, and France at their darkest hours, political machinations in North Africa, the D-Day victory and the ones that followed, presenting a composite portrait of American soldiers who were not fighting for any ideological reasons but fighting only to get back home. In the end, they voiced strong misgivings about Allied plans for postwar occupation in war-torn Europe.

> *NYT* 10/27/46, p3. 850w
>
> *SRL* 11/9/46, p19. 1050w

Miller, Max. *Daybreak for Our Carrier*. New York: McGraw, 1944. 184p

Less a battle story (which, according to one reviewer, is "no blood-and-thunder thriller. No desperate enemy attack is beaten back. There is little opposition over the target. Most of the fliers get back safely. No mock heroics are introduced"), it is more a manual of life and routine aboard a representative flattop, being a study as characteristic in reportage, art, and purpose as the finest efforts of the 1930s documentaries. It celebrates the power and efficiency of a carrier and its crew, in simple and quiet stem-to-stern vignettes of men at war as "thousand-thousandth(s) part of the ship . . . the same as rivets." Miller provides the reader with comforting assurance that the nation is in good mechanical and human hands. With contrived yet apt and effective symbolization, Miller indulges the metaphor of "a vessel so immense that her arms reach hundreds of miles from her body. The air is as much her realm as the sea. Clouds are as important to her as depth or currents. She is, in brief, a sort of fourth-dimensional creation. She is both bird and barque. She is a new *thing*!"

　NYT 6/4/44, p6. 550w

　WBR 6/18/44, p4. 550w

———. *The Far Shore*. New York: McGraw, 1945. 193p

An account of the Normandy invasion told from the vantage of one whose job it was to help land assault troops on the French coast and then to see that they were supplied with everything they needed. According to Lt. Commander Miller, to establish a beachhead against formidable enemy resistance required planning, decent weather, hard work, determination, and a coordinated effort between the army and the navy.

　SRL 7/28/44, p32. 700p

　WBR 4/23/45, p4. 900w

———. *It's Tomorrow Out Here*. New York: McGraw, 1945. 186p

Sketchy, subjective record of what it feels like to be stuck on a South Pacific island for a long, long time after the fighting had stopped and the battles moved elsewhere. Miller explores the lives of men in supply dumps, air bases, hospital wards, and recreation camps, where boredom is given the name "coral happy." There are photos of Seabees building airplane runways; Seabees dynamiting ice in the Attu Islands; Seabee carpenters building quonset huts; Seabees building pipelines from inland bases to piers; Seabees erecting a 90-foot radio mast! Still, "Even one's daily or nightly work will be monotonous, and [everyone] will be convinced that the war has moved on and left him. . . . He will begin to feel useless, no matter how hard he works. . . . He is, in brief, just one more guy who is becoming 'coral happy.' . . . Others are seeing action . . . others are going home, others are getting around. But he stays and is nothing." Much of Miller's narrative is like this. It fluctuates between straightforward reporting and editorializing. In his Author's Note at the front of the book, he indicates his approach: "Now that the Pacific War is ended, the book is designed not so much as a war book as a book of memories."

> *Springfield Republican* 12/16/45, p4. 144p
>
> *WBR* 12/23/45, p6. 250w

———. *The Lull*. New York: McGraw, 1946. 144p

Tells of the period immediately following the end of the hostilities and the return to civilian life, a "lull" in which the veteran endures a moody period of rehabilitation. This is truly a subjective stream-of-consciousness narrative of the personal conversion of a professional writer, lately a war correspondent, to civilian life.

> *WBR* 12/8/46, p24. 800w

Miller, Merle, and **Abe Spitzer**. *We Dropped the A-Bomb*. New York: Crowell, 1946. 152p

The radio operator of the *Great Artiste*, which carried the bomb to Nagasaki, tells of the solemn horror the crew felt about the destruction they inflicted on the city's civilian population when they dropped the bomb.

> *SRL* 9/21/46, p14. 550w
>
> *WBR* 8/25/46, p14. 400w

Miller, Norman. *I Took the Sky Road*. New York: Dodd, 1945. 212p

An account of Miller's career from his days at Annapolis to when he commanded a Liberator Squadron, which managed to sink and damage 66 Japanese ships, destroy 15 enemy planes, and wreck numerous enemy shore installations.

> *NYT* 8/19/45, p5. 800w
>
> *WBR* 8/19/45, p13. 550w

Milne, Caleb. *I Dream of the Day*. New York: Longmans, 1945. 122p

Collection of letters, 1942–1943, written by an American ambulance driver with the British Eighth Army from the North African war zone, containing reflections and perceptions of a young man trying to understand matters of life and death: "I don't understand life," he wrote before he was killed in May 1943, "so naturally death seems very simple to me." His first letter attempts to explain why he volunteered: "I'm not sure of the reasons [except] the ultimate agonies of war are, to me, not unconnected to Cavalries over the world [made] of a thousand hates and greeds." All around he witnesses the ugliness of war, but he records glimpses of beauty as well: dawn over the desert, a book on Mozart dropped by a wounded German soldier with the words *mehr licht* inscribed—more light!

> *BW* 9/16/45, p6. 650w
>
> *NYT* 9/16/45, p4. 500w

Mitchell, Robert, and **S. T. Tyng**. *The Capture of Attu. Infantry Journal*, 1944. 217p

The fighting in the Aleutians is told by Lt. Mitchell from accounts of the soldiers who fought the battles.

Mitchell, Ruth. *Serbs Choose War*. Gaarden City, N.Y.: Doubleday, 1943. 265p

A controversial attempt by the sister of Billy Mitchell to straighten out the tangle of ethnic components (Serbs, Croats, Slovenes, Armenians / Catholics, Moslems, Jews) that made up the Peoples Liberation Army fighting to ensure the independence and freedom of Yugoslavia. This is the story of the four years Mitchell spent in the Balkans, and her 13 months in German concentration camps and prisons because of her activities on behalf of the guerrillas.

> *NR* 10/2/43, p494. 500w
>
> *NYT* 10/17/43, p26. 900w

Moats, Alice-Leone. *Blind Date with Mars*. Garden City, N.Y.: Doubleday, Doran, 1943. 486p

Blending purely personal experiences with notations of current world history, neither deeply analytical, Moats details her extensive travels through the Far East, Russia, and the Middle East between August 1940 and March 1942. There are vivid descriptions of Moscow before the start of hostilities with Germany and military personnel stranded there when war broke out, as well as the utter calm of the Russian people in the momentous crisis. "As I walked along the streets, I was struck by the general air of serenity."

> *WBR* 2/12/42, p6. 1500w

———. *No Passport for Paris*. New York: Putnam, 1945. 275p

An account of reporter Moats' year in Spain and three weeks in France and Paris in April 1944 armed with a false passport. One reviewer suggested that the book displays more human rather than political interest, and he found peculiar the author's naïve attempt to depict the collaborators, fascists, and totalitarian-minded that she mingled among as "just plain folks, after all, and one should not be squeamish about them." Moats tells of attending a Paris dinner party where one of the guests was a German diplomat; enjoying black-market meals at elegant restaurants; meeting, at certain risk to herself, a downed American pilot being smuggled out of France by the underground.

> *Nation* 6/30/45, p724. 300w

NYT 5/27/45, p3. 650w

Moen, Lars. *Under the Iron Heel.* Philadelphia: Lippincott, 1941. 354p
The author, an American journalist, stranded for several months in Antwerp by the German invasion, provides an eyewitness account of the condition in an occupied country, including a searching study of the Belgian state of mind, German "friendly" tactics, and the character and behavior of the German soldier, all of which reflect the psychological side of war.
NR 3/31/41, p445. 1200w
NYT 3/9/41, p4. 1700w

Monaghan, Forbes. *Under the Red Sun: A Letter from Manila.* New York: Macmillan, 1946. 279p
Father Monaghan, a Jesuit priest, tells the story of how the largest religious mission in the world, made up of American and Filipino priests, conducted themselves during the Japanese occupation of the Philippines. Allowed virtual freedom by the conquerors, the Jesuits secretly aided Americans who escaped prison camps, providing food and shelter until they were able to join guerrilla fighters in the mountains.
WBR 11/24/46, p6. 500w

Monks, John Cherry. *Ribbon and a Star: The Third Marines at Bougainville.* New York: Holt, 1945. 245p
An anecdotal account of experiences of Marine officers and men in action by the author of *Brother Rat*, whose characters from the play come alive as real-life fighters in a grim jungle world. At one point, after a typical dialogue between two sober counterparts of his dramatic invention, Monks lays down a seething barrage of bitter criticism against "those on the outside who fight the war vicariously through books . . . will learn only a part of this great world story . . . and those who refuse to help won't learn much about the war. . . . The selfish few who work the angles, scorn the idealists . . . will learn nothing about men, nothing about courage, nothing about tempered steel friendship. . . . Only the fighting man though he may never tell—only he will know the truth."
NYT 11/25/45, p7. 950w
WBR 11/25/45, p3. 800w

Moore, Thomas. *The Sky Is My Witness.* New York: Putnam, 1943. 135p
In a fragmented manner, a young Marine dive-bomber pilot tells of his training, his girl, his experiences in action at Midway and the Solomons, his battle wound, and his homecoming.
BW 9/5/43, p3. 650w

Morrill, John, and **Pete Martin**. *South from Corregidor*. New York: Simon & Schuster, 1945. 252p

> Story revealing the heroic qualities that brought 17 men working together for 31 days on a 36-foot mine sweeper, *Quail*, through "the fiery furnace of Cavite and the slowly closing steel trap that was Bataan and Corregidor [while] navigating Japanese infested seas."
>
> > *NYT* 4/4/43, p3. 1100w
> >
> > *WBR* 4/4/43, p5. 550w

Morris, Colton, and **Hugh Cave**. *Fightin'est Ship*. New York: Dodd, 1944. 192p

> Narrative of the battle fought by a ship dubbed "the fightin'est" and the brave men who bore stifling heat, terrible tensions, the physical strain of action, and casualties suffered when she was sent to the bottom by the Japanese.
>
> > *SRL* 7/22/44, p25. 450w
> >
> > *WBR* 7/11/44, p6. 500w

Morris, Frank. *Pick Out the Biggest*. Boston: Houghton, 1943. 138p

> A seagoing correspondent mostly tells about a single battle that lasted little more than a quarter of an hour, in which the cruiser *Boise*, with the help of other American ships, inflicted heavy damage on six enemy vessels in and around the waters of the Solomon Islands, sinking most.
>
> > *NYT* 8/15/43, p5. 800w
> >
> > *WBR* 8/15/43, p3. 800w

Mowrer, Lillian. *Arrest and Exile*. New York: Morrow, 1941. 274p

> The story of Olga Kochanska, an American woman, who was arrested by the Soviet police and suffered a harrowing experience as a prisoner for six months in Siberia, until the arrival of her U.S. passport secured her release. Before that, with some 600 other "passengers," she was caught up in a "systematic dispersal of the Polish population, particularly the most influential and wealthy classes"— doctors, lawyers, rabbis, musicians—being transported by cattle-car trains to concentration camps.
>
> > *NYT* 12/2/41, p10. 850w
> >
> > *Springfield Republican* 10/26/41, p7. 1050w

Muehe, John. *American Sahib*. New York: Day, 1946. 242p

> The opinions of an American Field Service officer with the British Indian army during the war, casting the English in India as unwanted, and expressing sympathy for India's desire for independence. In tourist-like rendering, he records his glimpses of Indian life—emaciated children, students protesting the caste system, coolies smashing boulders into gravel for road construction, and much more of India's ambience under imperialistic British domination.

NYT 12/1/46, p52. 1100w

WBR 11/17/46, p32. 800w

Murphy, Mark. *Eighty-Three Days: The Survival of Seaman Izzi.* New York: Dutton, 1943. 124p

Mostly in the words of Seaman Bazil Izzi, Murphy tells the story of survivors from a torpedoed ship, drifting 83 days clinging to a flimsy raft before rescue finally came. Typical of some other survivor tales, it tells of jumping into the water as the sinking ship listed, the U-boat surfacing, and the German crew telling the men which way to find land. Managing to catch fish and birds, trapping drinking water in the rain, they were determined to live. Of the five men drifting so long a time, two died, and one of the three who remained crawled over to where Izzi lay and whispered, "These other fellows may give up, but *we* won't."

BW 9/26/43, p6. 650w

NYT 9/19/43, p23. 750w

Murrow, Edward R. *This Is London.* New York: Simon & Schuster, 1941. 237p

Carefully selected talks from Murrow's many London radio broadcasts over the period of August 1939 to December 1940, the upshot of which is an admiring depiction of the English character in the crucible of war.

Books 4/17/41, p3. 750w

NYT 4/13/41, p5. 440w

Mydans, Shelley. *The Open City.* Garden City, N.Y.: Doubleday, 1945. 245p

Not a factual journal but a novelized account with significant documentary relevance of the routine day-to-day life in Manila's internment camp, Santo Tomas, after the Japanese conquered the Philippines. The author, a photographer for *Life*, was imprisoned with her correspondent husband for eight months before being repatriated to the United States.

Nance, Ellwood, ed. *Faith of Our Fighters.* Christian Books, 1944. 304p

Book focuses on chaplaincy and the place of religion in the armed forces. Most pertinent are sections dealing with expressions of faith at camps and on battlefields; it also reports on visits to the fronts by four religious leaders—among them Archbishop Spellman and Dr. W. B. Pugh—who discuss "confessions of faith from camp and battlefield." Closing comments are offered by Vice President Henry Wallace.

NYT 12/24/44, p9. 500w

Neary, Bob. *Stalag Luft III: Sagan . . . Nuernberg . . . Moosburg*. North Wales, Penn.: Privately printed, 1946. 52p

A collection of German prison camp sketches, with descriptive text, based on the personal experiences of Lt. Bob Neary. "Camp Air Three" was one of the many throughout Germany built to house American airmen know as "Kriegies"—a contraction of the German word *Kriegsgefangenen*, meaning prisoner of war. The author tells the story of how more than 10,000 "despairing men" managed to survive on scant food rations and days of boredom before being liberated by General Patton's tank battalion. A secondary hardship of the camp was the prevalence of fleas, bedbugs, and lice in unbelievable numbers that manifested themselves at night. "Their bites covered every exposed part of the body, including the nose and eyelids." On the other hand, descriptions of life behind barbed wire as well as the visual images provided by 20 appealing line drawings tell something of a different story. Regular Red Cross parcels with supplies of cheese, corned beef, powdered milk, meat roll, and fruits were delivered regularly to the camp, as was a variety of sports equipment such as volleyballs, softballs and bats, boxing gloves, even ice skates sent by the YMCA, making imprisonment bearable. German guards sometimes provided censored American movies to be shown, and they distributed seeds for the prisoners to grow vegetable gardens. But "boredom and monotony were the prisoners' greatest enemies," their "Barbed Wire Disease." Combating it took a good deal of American ingenuity and comrade cooperation: through all kinds of sports, hobbies, amateur theatricals, band concerts (with instruments from the YMCA), and publishing camp newsletters and a weekly paper—all of which helped to maintain a decent level of morale among the men.

Nelson, David. *Journey to Chungking*. Minneapolis, Minn.: Augsburg, 1945. 154p

The author's "journey" confines itself to the trip from America to Chungking, China, via Australia and India. As representative of a coalition of Christian churches in the United States and Canada, Dr. Nelson was given the authority to act as a link between the home people and the missionaries in China. "The financial aid sent to the orphaned missions in China is indeed a tangible evidence that the Church heeds our Lord's commandment: 'Go ye therefore, and teach all nations,' even in a time when the world is torn by war" (foreword). Most of the book covers Nelson's 30-day journey overseas—on planes, transport ships, and military vehicles—with stopover impressions of Bombay life and the "Indian political puzzle." The last third of the narrative is centered in Chungking, a "city . . .

laid flat by Japanese bombings." Still, Nelson reports that "Chungking stores are stacked high with all kinds of merchandise. . . . There does not seem to be much rationing. . . . If you have the cash, you can buy anything." On the whole, the author offers a positive assessment of the situation: Schools continued in session uninterrupted. Business was booming. "Nothing disturbs the industrious Chunkingites," he writes. Two things, however, dismayed Nelson: "the sewage stench noticeable everywhere" and "the thousands and thousands of young men who roam the streets," having bribed their way out of being conscripted to fight in the nation's behalf," exhibiting "little idea of the war their country is waging."

Nelson, William, ed. *We Escaped.* New York: Macmillan, 1941. 258p

Twelve stories of individuals who fled from the tyranny of Nazi Germany and Fascist Spain to seek refuge in the United States have been translated into English in a restrained manner, avoiding melodrama and sentimentality. In a few cases the accounts were written by refugees themselves.

>   *NYT* 4/6/41, p9. 700w
>
>   *SRL* 5/31/41, p15. 500w

Newcomb, Ellsworth. *Brave Nurses.* New York: Appleton-Century, 1945. 176p.

Heroic nurses from America (and other lands) dramatize the courage of women who care for the wounded while braving the dangers of war. Photographs complement the text, showing nurses at work at sea and on land.

>   *SRL* 9/8/45, p33. 320w
>
>   *WBR* 9/23/45, p31. 230w

Newman, Bernard. *Balkan Background.* New York: Macmillan, 1945. 354p

Intimate portraits of Balkan peasants attempt to delineate the ethnic and cultural differences among the many peoples who inhabit that part of Europe, while advancing suggestions for the establishment of a peaceful federation of cooperating states after the war. Political speculations with a suggestion that things might be managed with the adoption of practical principles leading to a Balkan Charter.

>   *Current History* 2/45, p151. 1500w
>
>   *SRL* 1/27/45, p28. 950w

Newman, William. *Escape in Italy.* University of Michigan Press, 1945. 48p

Lt. Newman tells of being captured early in the action around Anzio beachhead, describing the generally decent treatment from the German guards. It didn't take Newman long to discover ways and means to engineer an escape, and soon he managed to do just that.

He was befriended by an Italian farmer and given food, drink, and a temporary place to hide. Eventually he made his way to Rome. His odyssey like the Italian countryside, had its ups and downs, days and nights winding in and around German command posts. Virtually everywhere he went he was taken in by an Italian family and given sanctuary. After a while, he took to walking the streets, even boldly taking "a lady out" for dinner at a public restaurant where German Gestapo sometimes ate. "Every waiter and every bartender in the better places in Rome knew that [I was an] escaped prisoner. They . . . did not betray [me]." His adventure ended when the Allies dislodged the Germans from southern Italy and entered Rome.

Norman, Charles. *A Soldier's Diary*. New York: Scribner, 1944. 51p

In a slender volume of short lyrics, the author, a typical American who volunteered at the age of 38, writes of the war from the viewpoint of an enlisted man. His poems cover many moods, mirroring the effect of army life upon a sensitive individual, while describing the memories and dreams of the ordinary soldier.

Springfield Republican 5/31/44, p6. 300w

Norton-Taylor, Duncan. *With My Heart in My Mouth*. New York: Coward-McCann. 1944. 167p

Tells how men live on warships and on battlefields, and how they fight, with a close-up report describing the Battle of Kula Gulf.

NYT 5/28/44, p28. 200w

SRL 6/10/44, p11. 850w

————. *I Went to See for Myself.* Heinemann, 1945. 156p

As an overseas correspondent riding on a naval destroyer, the author was a witness to several actions against the Japanese in the Pacific, from the assaults in the Solomons to a submarine chase and finally to the Battle of Kula Gulf with mixed feelings of trepidation and excitement.

O'Donnell, John. *Dear Joe*. Desaulniers, 1945. 170p

A book of letters includes those written by John O'Donnell to a mythical serviceman and those received in reply. From the starting date of August 7, 1942, until the Sunday of V-J Day, September 2, 1945, "Dear Joe" letters had reached approximately two-and-a-quarter-million words. In this book are reprinted the letters to and from the men and women in service, from countries in the European theater, from islands in the Pacific, and from camps and cities in the United States, along with the pictures of some 512 men and women who wrote them. The purpose behind the original printing of these letters in the *Davenport Democrat and Leader* was to inform the many men and women scattered all over the globe about what their comrades and friends in service were doing, and where they were doing it. The soldier in the Aleutians heard about the soldier in North Africa; the sailor in the Marshalls learned about the sailor in the North Sea; the Marines in Guadalcanal read about the Merchant Marines off the coast of France, the Waves, Wacs, Spars, and Lady Marines, along with military nurses, found out about the job each was doing.

Oechsner, Frederick, et al. *This Is the Enemy.* Boston: Little, 1942. 364p

Oechsner and four other American correspondents wrote parts of this account while they were interned in a German prison at the outbreak of war with the United States. Divided into four sections— "War, the Men Who Made It," "The Technique of War," "The War in Germany," "The War Abroad"—it adds up to an informative survey about the Third Reich in 1942.

NYT 11/15/42, p6. 800w

Oelschlager, Don, and **Stanley Tuell**. *The Story of the USS* Highlands. Santa Monica, 1946. 32p

The object of this "booklet" is to provide a lasting remembrance of the part the crew of an APA ship played in the victory against Japan. "The APA was born in the early days of World War II. The [first] 'A' means Auxiliary; 'P' Personnel; 'A' Assault; combined, these words spell transportation, supply and invasion. En route to the target the APA is a tenement, a means of transportation and a weapon of war. Upon arrival at the scene of action, the ship becomes a means of supply—men, guns and materials, the spearhead of the attack and a draft board of operational plans and strategy. When the essentials of war have been landed, the APA is immediately transposed into a clinic for the sick and a hospital for the wounded" (preface). The story details the beginning of the ship's training maneuvers off the California coast to the part played in the bloody invasion of Iwo Jima, landing troops and supplies under heavy enemy fire, and receiving the wounded to be cared for by the doctors and corpsmen aboard. "The picture [at Okinawa] was pretty much the same . . . at Iwo Jima. The same smell of gunpowder, the same flares in the skies, the same thunderous explosions that came from the battlewagons lying close off the shores." The story reached its climax with the *Highlands* steaming into Tokyo Bay on V-J Day.

Okubo, Mine. *Citizen 13660.* New York: Columbia Press, 1944. 209p

A Japanese American artist tells the story of her personal experience while confined in a relocation center on the West Coast. Day-by-day details of the restrictive life in camp from a minority citizen who considered herself 100% American but was denied treasured American freedom.

NYT 9/22/46, p7. 900w

WBR 10/13/46, p5. 1100w

Olds, Robert. *Helldiver Squadron*. New York: Dodd, 1944. 225p

Report on the experiences of the men and planes of the first navy Helldiver Squadron, from the initial battle at Rabaul, 11 November 1943—through the battles of Tarawa, the Marshalls, and Truk—to February 1944. Contains the honor roll of Squadron Seventeen.

BW 1/7/45, p6. 200w

O'Reilly, Tom. *Purser's Progress*. Garden City, N.Y.: Doubleday, 1944. 209p

A sports columnist for the tabloid *PM*, an "un-washed up" 38-year-old, became a "seagoing office boy" on a merchant freighter, wanting to do his bit in the war and hoping to derive personal satisfaction as a man by participating in a dangerous enterprise. O'Reilly's tale is a mix of serious moments, movingly told, sailing on a "Mulligan Stew" (mixed crew) Liberty Ship delivering cargo to battlefields, telling how the men behaved at sea and on shore. The closest O'Reilly gets to the dangers of his voyage came in a story told by Savannah, the black cook who had previously survived on a ship sunk by a torpedo: "It was January, an' cold. I swore I'd never go out again, but here I am."

NYT 6/4/44, p7. 440w

Osborn, Robert. *War Is No Damn Good*. Garden City, N.Y.: Doubleday, 1946. 96p

Through cartoons and captions, Osborn provides an angry, bitter, even savage look at war as a corrosive bad dream, filled with stupidities and frustrations.

San Francisco Chronicle 12/1/46, p2. 100w

Our Army at War. New York: Harper, 1944.

Signal Corps photographs give a somewhat sanitized visual history of the first two years of war from the Pacific to the Atlantic, from the Aleutians to North Africa, from France to Italy; 482 pictures.

BW 12/24/44, p4. 550w

WBR 10/8/44, p18. 550w

Our Flying Navy. New York: Macmillan, 1944. 97p

Eighty colored reproductions of paintings depict the training experiences of navy pilots and the later battles they were prepared to fight.

WBR 12/17/44, p2. 220w

Packard, Reynolds, and **Eleanor Packard**. *Balcony Empire: Fascist Italy at War*. New York: Oxford, 1942. 380p

Man and wife correspondents stationed in Italy write of their experiences when war broke out, especially reporting on the many months spent in concentration camps, along with items of assorted information—for example, how enemy submarines got past Gibraltar by hiding under neutral vessels. Included are stories about the genial Italian censors who cut into telephone conversations to make a joke or scrawled their comments on the margins of personal letters. Malcolm Cowley, the noted reviewer of the *New Republic*, wrote of its value as commentary on the Italian character in wartime.

  NR 11/23/42, 550w

Padover, Saul. *Experiment in Germany.* New York: Duell, 1946. 400p

As an American intelligence officer, Padover draws a number of conclusions about the mental climate of a defeated people based on conversations he had with Germans during the last stages of the war and after their country surrendered; horrified by the atrocities discovered yet assuaged by glimpses of decent feelings among some. He is also dismayed to become aware of widespread looting and even rapes by American men.

  NYT 4/14/46, p3. 1750w
  SRL 4/20/46, p10. 1900w

Page, Robert. *Air Commando Doc.* Akerman, 1946. 186p

The story of Lt. Colonel Page who organized a medical unit of doctors to accompany airmen to land troops from gliders onto a secret strip in the Burmese jungle, making a base from which to harass the Japanese and keep open the supply route to China.

  Springfield Republican 1/4/46, p4. 450w

Palmer, Edgard, ed. *G.I. Songs.* Dobbs Ferry, N.Y.: Sheridan, 1944. 253p

This collection of songs, written by men in the armed forces, runs the gamut from lighthearted to grouchy, from rowdy to fun—altogether conveying the feel of what being in the service was like. Some of the more popular marching songs and barracks ballads from World War I are included for comparative analysis.

  NYT 8/13/44, p12. 360w

Parris, John, and **Ned Russell**; in collaboration with **Leo Disher** and **Philip Ault.** *Springboard to Berlin.* New York: Crowell, 1943. 410p

Four correspondents of United Press give a chronological, sometimes overlapping, account of the American operations in the Mediterranean area, from the North African invasion to the landings in Sicily, pointing to the lessons learned by the army's mistakes in strategy and preparation—plenty of action and heroism.

  NYT 9/2/43, p34. 280
  SRL 10/3/43, p13. 1000w

Parsons, Robert. *Mob Three: A Hospital in the South Pacific Jungle.* Indianapolis, Ind.: Bobbs, 1945. 248p

Captain Parsons, a navy doctor, tells how he helped establish a fully equipped mobile care station far from the battle areas to provide efficient medical treatment to the men wounded in action. Part of the book deals with the natives on the island—their customs, houses, schools, churches, habits of work and play—which had interest for the Americans who lived among them.

BW 4/8/45, p8. 310w

WBR 3/11/45, p8. 750w

Paul, Louis. *Ordeal of Sgt. Smoot.* New York: Crown, 1943. 220p

Humorous sketches relating to the woeful trials and tribulations of a regular army sergeant doing his job of whipping into shape a most unpromising group of raw recruits.

Peabody, Polly. *Occupied Territory.* Cresset, 1941. 292p

Most of the book concerns Peabody's experiences in German-occupied France, reporting the feelings of the people—from Marshall Petain to a railway porter; from Vichy Premier Laval to a collaborationist innkeeper; from German authorities to growing underground resistance.

Peart, Cecil. *Peart's Journal.* Privately printed, 1946.

Prepared from notes kept on a prisoner-of-war odyssey from Bilibid Prison, Manila, P.I., to Manchukuo, via the prison ship *Oryoku Maru*, by Cecil J. Pearl, a pharmacist mate of the U.S. Navy, and presented by the author to the Hospital Corps archives for the Bureau of Medicine and Surgery. According to Ben F. Dixon, Lt. HC USN, archivist, "The story recounted . . . is one of the rare treasures to come from the prison camps." Peart has set down in matter-of-fact sentences the things which he saw, did, and experienced. All through the narrative the one thing he wrote about was "chow," and after chow came the terrible afflictions of the sick. When a shipmate or an officer used skulduggery to get more chow, Peart wrote about it. When he himself scraped the swill pails for a few extra grains of rice, he jotted it down. There was always "a terrible hunger and cold." Often "there wasn't enough space for lying down." Toilet facilities were nonexistent on the ships that carried internees from place to place. Prisoners had to defecate "like animals" over the side, "but the wind was so strong, the stools of others were blown all over." There was a never-ending struggle to keep clean and healthy, but sickness (colds, dysentery, sore throats, lice) was constant. The journal shows some evidence of editing, as Peart translated his hieroglyphic notes into words and phrases. Here and there, as he recalled items he had not originally jotted into the notebooks, he doubtless added to the original diary, processing his notes into a narrative of his experiences.

Pender, Kenneth. *Adventure in Diplomacy: Our French Dilemma.* New York: Dodd, 1945. 280p

As one of a group of officers sent as an observer to North Africa, Pender gives an insider's account of America's diplomacy in Algeria, a good portion of which is taken up with an attack on De Gaulle and Gaullism and a criticism of the American exploits against the Free French, including immediate as well as future U.S. relations with France.

> *SRL* 12/14/41, p7. 2000w
>
> *WBR* 12/16/41, p2. 1350w

Perry, George Sessions, and **Isabel Leighton**. *Where Away: A Modern Odyssey.* New York: McGraw-Hill, 1944. 249p

Excellent pen sketches by Coastguardsman John J. Floherty Jr. add to a perceptive narrative by authors of the strange odyssey from Pearl Harbor on the U.S. cruiser *Marblehead*, manned by an exemplary, close-knit crew. Not an eyewitness account, it is a narrative pieced together from the memories of men who survived (13 did not) enemy air attacks in the Java Sea. Badly damaged, the ship was repaired and returned to service a few months later.

> *NYT* 12/3/44, p7. 700w
>
> *WBR* 12/26/44, p4. 950w

Phelps, Harvey. *God's Deliverance from Nazi Hands.* American Bible Institute, 1943. 181p

When war came to France, Reverend Phelps was Dean of the European Christian Mission. As the German army advanced through the north of France, Phelps, along with thousands of refugees, fled from Paris as best he could. "Getting out of the city was not easy. On the principal streets leading from Paris [were] people with vehicles of every description: automobiles new and old, horse-drawn wagons, bicycles, pushcarts, wheel barrows, perambulators." When Phelps decided to return to Paris, he kept notes telling of the feelings of the French people about the occupation of their country by Nazis and their humiliating defeat. One chapter, entitled "Life and Work Under Nazi Rule," details the hardships endured by an occupied people. "One of the worst things we . . . suffered that winter was the standing in line for food on bitter cold days." Stringent rationing of food and fuel made daily living a challenge. For instance, it allowed "one egg a month" for each person. Through some misunderstanding and the excessive suspicion of the German Gestapo, Phelps was taken into custody, and much of the latter part of the book describes his "days and nights" locked in a dismal cell. Eventually, weakened and ill from lack of nutritious food, Phelps was released from prison and made his way out of conquered France to Spain and Portugal. This is a true glimpse of the early days of the German occupation, detailing the trials and tribulations of a man whose faith in God sustained him.

Phillips, Harry Irving. *All-out Arlene: A Story of the Girls behind the Boys behind the Guns*. Garden City, N.Y.: Doubleday, 1943. 202p

The experiences of Arlene Chrystal Applegate of Brooklyn and her family and pals, including her dog, in their all-out effort to win the war. Arlene ended up as a sergeant in the Wacs in Africa, where practically every other private and officer proposed to her, but Arlene was faithful to her hero, Terry.

NYT 7/18/43, p9. 750w

WBR 7/8/43, p18. 550w

Pratt, Fletcher. *Fleet Against Japan*; foreword by Admiral Nimitz. New York: Harper, 1946. 263p

After three introductory chapters on the ships of the navy and their commanders, Nimitz and Calaghan among them, Pratt recounts three sea offensives against Japan—at the Aleutians, the Marianas, and Leyte Gulf—U.S. victories that rank high in naval history.

SRL 5/11/46, p22. 950w

WBR 4/21/46, p12. 1040w

————. *Night Work*. New York: Holt, 1946. 267p

The story of Task Force 39 that was sent to the Solomons to slow the fast-moving Japanese offensive known as the "Tokyo Express." Comprised of four cruisers and a few destroyers, they succeeded in their mission. Tactical accounts of the battles are clearly explained, accompanied by helpful diagrams.

NR 3/11/46, p356. 480w

Prosser, David. *Journey Underground*. New York: Dutton, 1945. 347p

A young American pilot, who bailed out of his crippled plane over occupied France, managed—with the help of the French underground—to avoid capture by the enemy for nearly three months, after which he made it across the Pyrenees into Spain. Marked by the actions and feelings of the people who helped in his escape and survival.

SRL 11/3/45, p9. 320w

WBR 12/2/34, p26. 450w

Purcell, John. *Flights to Glory*. New York: Vanguard, 1944. 184p

The exploits of 40 fliers in various theaters of war are integrated in this book that is less a roster of heroes than an intelligent and critical discussion of the use of air power under all conditions. It is based on a sound knowledge of the design, function, and history of aircraft, which rounds out accounts of the individual flights to make a good history of the war in the air, with special emphasis on the Pacific theater.

SRL 5/113/44, p39. 50w

Putnam, Russell. *Sincerely Put: Letters to His Friends.* Louisville, Ky.: Privately printed, 1945. 285p

This is an unpretentious collection of personal letters to the "Dear Folks" at home, most of them receiving a vivid picture of the smell, feel, and look of war from a colonel who saw war at a distance and up close. Serving various missions from Egypt, Saudi Arabia, England, Normandy, and Paris, he offers homey impressions of high-ranking civilian and military officials, among them Roosevelt, Churchill, Chiang Kai-shek, King Farouk of Egypt, and King Peter of Yugoslavia. More an observer than a combatant, this allowed "Put" to describe the events and people that he witnessed "sincerely." Typical is his commentary during the early days of the Normandy invasion: "One can't be too sure [the French] are too happy about these Americans coming into their country . . . regardless of how much we brag about 'liberating' them. For we have brought a lot of death and destruction with us. . . . The Germans didn't have to 'blast' their way into Normandy, it fell into their hands. We can hardly expect these people to take the philosophic 'long-range view' when their relatives have been killed by our bombs, their houses wrecked by our gun fire. They do not show any dislike, so far as I saw. Neither do they greet us with cheers." The final episode is especially interesting in that it deals with the sad problem of "shell shock" or "battle fatigue" in a most compassionate manner: "It was heartbreaking to listen to these boys . . . they had suffered the tortures of hell . . . they had proved their courage under the most dangerous, trying conditions . . . yet their greatest worry was that they thought they had failed. They seemed to feel that now, since they could no longer take combat, they had proved to be cowards. They wanted to go back to combat . . . even though that was what they feared most . . . and they knew they were no longer capable of carrying on."

Pyle, Ernest. *Ernie Pyle in England.* New York: McBride, 1941. 228p

Human-interest sketches of cockney waitresses, shipyard longshoremen, Welsh miners, railway porters, farmers he talked to as he traveled throughout England and Scotland, meeting people on the streets and in the pubs, visiting them in their homes—summing up the reactions of Britons to the war.

NYT 8/31/41, p4. 430w

———. *Here Is Your War.* New York: Holt, 1943. 304p

Human-interest story of the African campaign consisting of the author's newspaper columns in expanded form, with pen-and-ink drawings added. Pyle says: "I haven't written anything about the 'Big Picture' because I don't know anything about it. I only know what we see from our worms-eye view, and our segment of the picture consists only of tired and dirty soldiers who are alive and don't want to die; of long silent men wandering back down the hill from battle . . . of jeeps and petrol dumps and smelly bedding rolls and C rations and cactus patches and blown bridges and dead mules and hospital tents and shirt collars greasy black from months of wearing; and of laughter, too, and anger and wine and lovely flowers and constant cussing. All these it is composed of; and of graves and graves and graves." Book covers every conceivable experience in war, from infantry mascots to stretcher bearers, from bomber pilots to foot soldiers in foxholes, from scorching heat to freezing cold, totally defining the men who fought the war.

    NYT 10/31/43, p1. 1450w
    WBR 10/31/43, p2. 1000w

———. *Brave Men.* New York: Holt, 1944. 474p

Pyle presents what he refers to as "the grunt's eye view" of war, with all its squalor, discomfort, weariness, worry, fear, and homesickness, and in his travels he gets the men to tell him what they feel—doing a job they mostly hated but did nevertheless. Actually, Ernie Pyle's book added up to a statement about America's most precious meaning by maintaining a focus on people as human beings rather than the glamour of heroic action or grand principles for which the United States fought. Even when the deadliest battles took place, Pyle tried to keep his sights on the important things by not letting the so-called larger issues take over from the human concerns. Once he wrote, "When I sat down to write, I saw instead: men at the front suffering and wishing they were somewhere else, men in routine jobs just behind the lines bellyaching because they couldn't get to the front, all of them desperately hungry for somebody to talk to besides themselves, no women to be heroes in front of, damned little wine to drink, precious little song, cold and fairly dirty, just toiling from day to day in a world full of insecurity, discomfort, homesickness, and a dulled sense of danger."

    NYT 11/26/44, p1. 1400w
    SRL 11/25/44, p7. 1000w

———. *Last Chapter.* New York: Holt, 1946. 150p

Covers the experiences of Pyle's last assignment as a war correspondent where, during the battle of Okinawa, he was killed by a

Japanese sniper. Once again, he paints a word portrait of the average American serviceman, disposed to friendliness and a simple outlook on life, who in the heat of battle can summon the tough and necessary ruthlessness required by war.

  NYT 6/2/46, p3. 1500w
  SRL 6/1/46, p13. 1250w

Raff, Edson. *We Jumped to Fight.* New York: Duell, 1944. 207p
Story of an American infantryman who became a paratrooper and an account of the first U.S. airborne unit in action. The battalion's jump in Tunisia took place with enough mixture of strategy, daring skill, and luck to make it succeed in holding a vital airfield and a communications center against superior enemy resistance.

  BW 7/9/44, p6. 170w
  NYT 7/2/44, p1. 900w

Rainear, Charles. *We Are of Clay.* Boston: Houghton, 1945. 95p
Letters and random jottings of Lt. "Chick" Rainear, who did his job as a P-38 fighter pilot—but wondered why. Curious note of fatalism seeps into most of what Rainear has to say.

Raleigh, John. *Behind the Nazi Front.* New York: Dodd, 1941. 307p
An eyewitness account by a *Chicago Tribune* journalist of life and politics in wartime Berlin, underscoring the severity of life in the capital along with the fragility of civilian stamina.

————. *Pacific Blackout.* New York: Dodd, 1943. 244p
Raleigh describes the approach and arrival of war in Java and Australia, both from secondhand accounts as well as from his own witness, remarking especially on the morale factor of the Dutch and native people in the region.

  WBR 4/18/43, p17. 1000w

Rathbone, Alfred. *He's in the Subbusters Now.* New York: McBride, 1944. 224p
Story of the so-called sub-busters, the small navy warships built especially for antisubmarine patrol. Mostly for young readers, illustrated with official navy photographs. The best part of the book describes firing-range drills, small boat handling, and swimming lessons.

  Springfield Republican 1/13/44, p5. 330w

Rawlings, Charles. *We Saw the Battle of the Atlantic.* New York: Pickwick. Sixty-three pages with black-and-white photographs and five color photographs.
From a reporter and a cameraman aboard the *Diana*, a Coast Guard cutter sailing under navy orders, on the lookout for enemy submarines during the crucial battle along the eastern seaboard of the United States. With a crew of five officers and fifty men, the small

ship patrolled the area around Hatteras nicknamed "Periscope Lane" and "Torpedo Junction," where the U-boat fleet "was having [its] fun" sinking Allied cargo vessels. The problem was that "there were . . . not enough of our Navy's ships to do much [against] them." Once, after dodging an enemy torpedo, the *Diana* took the offensive with depth charges, "waiting for some sign that the sub was dead." Sounding the strength-in-diversity theme again, Rawlings announced that "there were men in our crew from Michigan, Missouri, North Carolina, Massachusetts, the District of Columbia, Wisconsin, Kansas, Georgia, Pennsylvania, West Virginia, Maryland, New Jersey, Alabama, Virginia, Illinois, Louisiana, Mississippi, Maine, Texas, Kentucky, New York, Washington, and Nebraska."

Read, Francis. *G.I. Parson.* Harrisburg, Penn.: Morehouse-Gorham, 1945. 117p

Tells of the author's ministering for three years at home, abroad, on the high seas, in training camps, on maneuvers, in battle zones, giving counsel, and material and spiritual guidance to the healthy and sick, the wounded and dying, regardless of religious affiliation—Catholic, Protestant, Jew, Mormon. "I never asked the soldier his faith. . . . He never asked me mine." Several bloody battles on Attu and Kwajalein are graphically described, with Read remarking that "with two campaigns under their belts, the men of the Seventh had no illusions about the glories of war."

Redding, John, and **Harold Leyshon**. *Skyways to Berlin.* Indianapolis, Ind.: Bobbs, 1943. 290p

Samples of the achievements of American airmen in England who told their experiences to two press-relations officers attached to the Eighth Air Force. A soup-to-nuts anecdotal account ranging from stories of canned meat in mess halls and softball games on the London Commons, to missions over the hottest spots of Hitler's fortress Europe.

> *NYT* 9/12/43, p1. 1200w
> *SRL* 9/25/43, p5. 700w

Redmond, Juanita. *I Served on Bataan.* Philadelphia: Lippincott, 1943. 167p

Not only is this a woman's perspective on the battles of Bataan and Corregidor, but it is also the story of what nurses endured during the first few months of war in the Pacific while working in improvised jungle hospitals and underground wards to care for the wounded.

> *BW* 3/14/43, p2. 600w
> *WBR* 3/14/43, p3. 1040w

Reynolds, Quentin. *The Wounded Don't Cry*. New York: Dutton, 1941. 253p

As a witness to the German bombing in London, Reynolds pays tribute to the indomitable spirit of the British people—unconquered, undiscouraged, still laughing—learned by talking to all sorts of men and women to find out what they think and how they feel. One purpose of the book was to underscore the brutality of the bombings and strafing of the clog of slow-moving refugees on the roads and bridges of the countries being invaded by the Nazis.

Current History and Forum 3/41, p36. 900w

NYT 1/26/41, p12. 700w

————. *A London Diary*. New York: Random House, 1941. 304p

An "uncensored" diary of an American foreign correspondent who admits to "never [having] had so much fun in my life," during the German Blitzkrieg, October to December 1940.

Books 5/4/41, p16. 400w

NYT 4/11/41, p12. 550w

————. *Convoy* (English title: *Don't Think It Hasn't Been Fun*). New York: Random House, 1942. 303p

The ostensible subject of the book—sailing on a freighter in a convoy bound for England over an Atlantic filled with marauding German U-boats—is paid very little attention, while most of the talk deals with personal reminiscences having nothing to do with the war and everything to do with happy days of long ago shared with friends from the sports and literary worlds.

Books 2/8/42, p12. 500w

NYT 3/15/42, p20. 600w

————. *Only the Stars Are Neutral*. New York: Random House, 1942. 300p

Report of experiences during the winter of 1941–1942, in London, Moscow, Cairo. The work is long on personal impressions and "adventures" and short on political analysis. While some of the book gives an account of battles in North Africa, the best parts deal with the life a journalist had to lead—either in a Russian town under Nazi siege or a little desert outpost in Libya.

Books 6/21/42, p3. 850w

NYT 6/30/42, p4. 800w

————. *Dress Rehearsal*. New York: Random House, 1943. 278p

From the vantage of a British battleship, Reynolds provides an eyewitness account of the tragic raid on Dieppe, thought to be a dress rehearsal to an invasion on the Continent. Filled with amusing anecdotes, this is less a military narrative and more a human-interest picture of commando fighters.

NYT 3/14/43, p3. 850w

———. *The Curtain Rises.* New York: Random House, 1944. 353p

The chapter "D-Day: Italy" is the most serious piece of reporting in the volume, otherwise the book is a virtual autobiography of the life and times of Quentin Reynolds and those of his correspondent colleagues in wartime Europe. It is filled with reflections of their gripes and pleasures in between serious moments.

NYT 3/23/44, p7. 1250w

———. *70,000 to 1: The Story of Lt. Gordon Manuel.* New York: Random House, 1946. 217p

According to Reynolds, Master Sergeant Gordon Manuel of Hodgdon, Maine, was shot down over New Britain on the night of May 21, 1943, and was the sole survivor of a wrecked B-17. Eight-and-a-half months later he was rescued by a submarine. The most interesting part of the story tells of the affection and respect that developed between the downed flier and the natives who rescued him, in addition to worthwhile tips on how to survive in a jungle for many months. *Note:* There is some doubt if there ever was a Gordon Manuel and if this is a true wartime story.

SRL 7/29/46, p12. 600w

WBR 7/14/46, p5. 800w

Rickenbacker, Eddie. *Seven Came Through.* Garden City, N.Y.: Doubleday, 1943. 118p

A man-against-nature survival tale, recounting the ordeal of eight men whose Flying Fortress ran out of fuel and dumped them into the Pacific Ocean, thereafter a picture of strong-willed men battling against the elements and discouragement. Much of what the seven men (one did not survive) went through was typical of other survival stores: hunger, thirst, chilly nights, burning days, sporadic delirium, hopes occasionally bolstered by the sight of planes, catching a bird or a few fish with makeshift hooks, wringing rainwater into a pail from soaked clothing. The sort of Odyssean man Rickenbacker proves himself to be was shown in his determination to overcome all threats to their well-being and existence. Very simply, he would not allow the men to succumb to despair. Indeed, Rickenbacker himself, exhibiting a heroic self-confidence, stated that "there was no time that I lost faith in our ultimate rescue, but others did not seem to share this state of mind fully with me." Nonetheless, not only would he not allow himself to quit, he would not allow others to do so either, and by such determination the men who survived probably owed their lives to him.

BW 4/4/43, p3. 900w

NYT 3/21/43, p1. 1100w

Robertson, Ben. *I Saw England.* New York: Knopf, 1941. 213p

Impressions given by an American reporter for the New York tabloid *PM* about the reactions of the British people following the Nazi Blitzkrieg and bombs raining down from German aircraft on the city of London.

> *Books* 4/6/41, p5. 700w
>
> *NYT* 4/6/41, p5. 500w

———. *News of the Forty-Fifth.* University of Oklahoma Press, 1944. 158p

Helped by Bill Mauldin's art, these pieces originally published in the *Forty-Fifth Division News* are an "in house" miscellany written and published by the enlisted men of the Forty-Fifth Division of the United States Army. Reporting on the outfit's training period, journey overseas, and participation in the battles of Sicily and the Italian mainland, the book underscores in most items the wacky aspects of life in the division.

> *BW* 5/7/44, p4. 500w
>
> *NYT* 5/14/44, p5. 650w

Rogers, Edward. *Doughboy Chaplain.* Meador, 1946.

This account sets forth in brief fashion the experiences of a chaplain attached to an infantry battalion of the First Infantry Division of the U.S. Army. It covers a period of more than 37 months and tells a tale told by many other chaplains who similarly served the spiritual and emotional needs of troops in combat, particularly performing traditional religious services under the most informal conditions. As chaplain, Rogers saw things that assured him that the sacrifices made by the men would lead to a victory, and that the eventual peace would be stern for the enemy, yet just.

Romulo, Carlos. *I Saw the Fall of the Philippines.* Garden City, N.Y.: Doubleday, 1942. 323p

An account of the conditions on Bataan—besieged by a superior enemy force—and of the courage of Filipinos and Americans fighting together, bomb-wracked in foxholes, wondering if help was coming from the United States.

> *Books* 1/17/43, p1. 1850w
>
> *SRL* 1/16/43, p5. 1000w

———. *I See the Philippines Rise.* Garden City, N.Y.: Doubleday, 1946. 273p

A sequel to the author's *I Saw the Fall of the Philippines*, combining a mostly personal narrative on the effects the war had on him and his family with a broad appeal for the United States to recognize and reward the sufferings and struggles of the Filipinos under

Japanese occupation. Many Filipinos fought side-by-side with Americans at Bataan under General Wainwright.

    WBR 4/21/46, p3. 1000w

Rontch, Isaac, ed. *Jewish Youth at War.* Marstin, 1945. 304p

A book of letters written by Jewish men and women in every branch of service, on every front around the globe, from North Africa and Italy to the waters and islands of the South Pacific, from Alaska to Western Europe. They recount the experiences of bomber pilots and infantrymen, paratroopers and submariners, more often than not with a perspective of Jewish consciousness. At the same time, testifying to a world at mid-century significantly different than at century's end, it is surprising the number of passing and comfortable references to Christmas and that Christian holiday season besides Passover and Chanuka. Indeed, sentiments similar to "I hope we'll all be together again next Christmas" were not uncommon. M/Sgt. Joe Chandler celebrated Christmas with his comrades on a barge in the open sea; Marine Sgt. Sam Solomon on Tarawa wished his "Dear Mom . . . A Merry Christmas"; Cpl. Buddy Bier went to a Catholic Mass where he said the Lord's Prayer and sang Holy Night; Sgt. Arthur Lauren noted that "soon Christmas would be here with the men singing Christmas carols"; Lt. Carl Abrams wore a Catholic medal given to him by a French boy "for luck;" Sam Dooka, writing to the "Mother's Club," welcomed the "Christmas presents" they sent; Cpl. Leon Becker volunteered for KP to allow the Gentiles to enjoy Christmas, even though he was sad to pass up celebrating the holiday himself. As one soldier put it: "It's the little things in life that we fight and die for. Stuff like Mom's pie, the old school dances, Christmas." Other notable aspects were the lack of complaint in these letters, despite the hardships, homesickness, and dangers constantly endured, coupled with expressions of idealism concerning the hopes for a better world when the forces of darkness were defeated. "We cannot go forward when the evil hand of Nazism has blacked out the lives of so many millions of people." Overall, the letters touch on a variety of subjects: speculations about the war and tragedies in battle, nostalgic references to home and friends, human-interest stories, travelogues of exotic places worldwide, expressions of anger at the striking workers in war plants, dismay over race riots on American streets, and puzzlement over indications of growing apathy on the home front.

Rose, Don. *Diary of a Post War Correspondent.* Bryn Athyn, Penn.: Privately printed, 1945. 95p

A miscellany regarding: "Bombs in a Pickle Barrel," "Racketeers in Uniform," "The Valley of Death," "Rome Through a Keyhole,"

"Plush-Lined Foxhole," including Rose's speculation on whether Hitler died in Berlin.

Roy, Morris. *Behind Barbed Wire.* Kansas City, Kan. Richard Smith, 1946. 329p

"This book is an authentic record of and for those combat airmen in the European Theater of Operations who, as prisoners of war, were confined in Stalag Luft I, Barth, Germany. It was written there, the illustrations were drawn there, and the photographs taken there. It contains a Directory of the men confined in the camp, and their home addresses. . . . Part I comprises the stories of twelve flight missions that ended in disaster over enemy territory, each told by a participant who escaped death; and the experiences of 'Joe Flieger,' typical downed airman, from the moment of landing until he reached Barth—experiences which might well be a composite of those of the twelve narrators. . . . Their aircraft were struck by all kinds of enemy gunfire. They bailed out from every type of aircraft at every altitude; they crash-landed on every type of terrain known to man, as well as every body of water in the E.T.O. . . . The reception given these airmen immediately on landing in enemy or enemy-occupied territory varied according to the nationality, sex, and temperament of their greeters. Captured by the Germans, many airmen suffered atrocities, though the majority were treated respectfully and looked upon with awe and curiosity. In the enemy-occupied territory, members of the underground often risked their lives to help downed Allied airmen evade German capture. . . . As no work for the Reich could be required of the prisoners at Stalag Luft I, each day was borne only to be killed, a slow agonizing process. Out of almost nothing—if you leave out courage, initiative, ingenuity, humor, and an unalterable determination to outwit their captors and make more bearable the hard conditions of life there—the men of Stalag Luft I published a daily (underground) newspaper, produced plays, ran a library, wrote and illustrated this and other books, organized a glee club, wrote music, arranged a sports program and an exhibit of their handicraft, made clocks and clothing, improved their beds . . . baited their captors, and toward that chief aim of all, escape, utilized stray bits of glass, wire, wood, tin cans, cloth, and the like for tunnel-digging and disguise. All this and much more in a prison well guarded by barbed wire and Germans who were efficient watchmen and whose capricious interpretations of rules and the punishments stipulated for breaking them were never on the indulgent side. When one considers how readily such harsh incarceration might have embittered the wellspring of life for these men, and how the apparent hopelessness of escape, both physical and mental, might have diminished it to the vanishing point, the story of Barth is a tribute to that positive urge in liberty-bred men that inevitably seeks to cancel out the negative facts of imprisonment" (foreword).

Runbeck, Margaret. *The Great Answer*. Boston: Houghton, 1944. 239p

Brief sketches of men, women, and children in war who have turned to prayer in their hour of need and escaped dangers in battles, threats at sea, and terrors in occupied countries, proving to Runbeck that "man's extremity is God's opportunity" and that a belief in God, even though unacknowledged, is in back of every fighting man.

Springfield Republican 4/18/44, p6. 380w

Russell, William. *Berlin Embassy*. New York: Dutton, 1941. 307p
Firsthand impressions of wartime mentality in Berlin, of what life in the capital city felt like to the average person in the months between the invasion of Poland and the defeat of France, having to deal with unheated rooms and food shortages.

Books 10/19/41, p3. 700w

NYT 2/15/42, p3. 1050w

St. George, Thomas. *c/o Postmaster*. New York: Crowell, 1943.
Tells of young Americans stationed in Australia learning about fish and chips, tea and scones, ice cream that is an "ice," liquor referred to as "plonk," hard candy as "lollies," and the inconvenience of a shortage of Coca-Cola as well as female companionship, beer—which is rather a glorified strawberry pop—and the confusion in dealing with Australian money. The American soldiers are learning things from their Australian friends, and Australians are learning fast, in turn, from Americans.

———. *Proceed Without Delay*. New York: Crowell, 1945. 181p
Army life in Australia enjoyed by a combat correspondent on "per diem" status that provided room and board, which kept him free of army barracks and the mess hall. Mostly a book of humor, with cartoons by the author, about war in the rear area, far from combat, although in the closing pages of the book, St. George touches briefly on the grim business of the Leyte campaign, as he found himself crouched and full of fear in a foxhole as bombs and bullets exploded all around him.

SRL 7/21/45, p17. 400w

NYT 7/29/45, p6. 500w

St. John, Robert. *From the Land of the Silent People*. Garden City, N.Y.: Doubleday, 1942. 353p
Chronicle of "all that [he] saw and heard and smelled and just a bit of what he thought" as an eyewitness to the German campaign in

the Balkans and the terrible price which ordinary people in Yugoslavia and Greece paid for living in small, weakly armed countries.
St. John tells about the horror of Nazi warfare that "makes no sense
to me." His narrative is a grim factual report that begins from the
day Serbian nationalists rebelled at a compact signed by Prince Paul
and ends when the author manages to get to Egypt.

  NR 2/16/42, p244. 1200w

  NYT 1/8/42, p9. 1050w

St. Joseph, R. *Leyte Calling.* New York: Vanguard, 1945. 320p

The true story of an American soldier who eluded capture when the
Japanese conquered the Philippines and lived in hiding on Leyte and
Mindanao for more than two years among people loyal to the
United States, participating with them in their guerrilla warfare
against the enemy.

  SRL 3/10/45, p28. 850w

  WBR 2/18/45, p5. 800w

Sayre, Joel. *Persian Gulf Command.* New York: Random House,
1945. 140p

The difficulties and achievements of a noncombat battalion of truck
drivers, railroaders, stevedores, and other service troops doing a
tough job of getting war supplies to Russia through terrible heat and
over the difficult terrain of Iran. Part of the book is a history of the
Persian Gulf area, from ancient times to the present, including social
and religious customs. Mostly it is filled with anecdotes about the
noncombatant service troops, detailing the boredom suffered and
the diversions offered by the whirling dervishes of Iran, occasional
USO shows, and writing censored love letters to girls back home.

  NYT 9/2/45, p5. 1050w

Schacht, Alexander. *G.I. Had Fun.* New York: Putnam, 1945. 136p

The clown prince of baseball, pantomimist Al Schacht, tells of his
experience while entertaining the troops overseas with his one-man
show, meanwhile learning that most of the soldiers knew more
about batting averages and baseball history than he did, that one of
their ambitions when they got home was to buy a farm or a jeep,
and that the pin-up business is just press-agent stuff.

  BW 7/1/45, p4. 130w

Schmidt, Albert. *Al Schmidt, Marine.* New York: Norton, 1944. 142p

Story of an average young American who joined the Marines,
fought heroically on Guadalcanal, was blinded in battle, and returned home after a long period of recuperation and therapy, only to
fight a harder battle against the blues and for personal acceptance of
his permanent disability and a restoration of whatever wholeness
was possible—a fight that he ultimately wins.

NYT 2/27/44, p10. 500w

Schubart, William. *From the Letters of William Howard Schubart, Jr.*
Stamford, Conn.: Overbrook Press, 1946. 108p

In letters to family members and friends, Schubart exhibits a typical
impatience with the war for keeping him away from home, a girl, a
job, and living "a standard run-of-the-mill existence . . . more or less
Sinclair Lewis-Americanish sort of life, while at the same time being glad to be a part of the 'game' of war which had a romantic
quality about it. . . . There is danger from time to time, but there is a
real sense of accomplishment," he wrote to his father. Yet, he wrote
to a friend explaining that "rattling around the world . . . is supposed
to be a romantic business, and will probably seem colorful as hell in
retrospect, but while you're actually [doing it], it can be wearying,
brother, wearying beyond words." Otherwise, the letters are filled
with references to war and peace, military and civilian life, school,
work, writing ambition, George Gershwin and Irving Berlin tunes,
homesickness, democracy, and a scathing complaint about striking
union war workers: "I'd like to go back home and find a Union or-
ganizer and kick his ——— teeth out. . . . [Workers] ought to have
to sweat a little harder so as to increase production and get our
sweating over here over a little quicker." However, Schubart
quickly forgot his "petty" irritations about union betrayals of the
troops and yearned "to get into at least one good stiff sea-fight" and
taste "a good whiff of battle smoke." Schubart and 171 officers and
men were killed when a newly commissioned destroyer, *Cooper*,
engaged parts of the Japanese navy around the Philippines and was
sunk by enemy torpedoes. Several accounts of this action are ap-
pended to his book of letters.

Scott, Robert. *God Is My Co-Pilot.* New York: Scribner, 1943. 277p

Primary interest in the book comes from the reports of fighting the
Japanese in the China–Burma sector of the war under the command
of General Chennault, with episodes of daring adventure, necessary
resourcefulness, and individual courage woven with details about
air battle tactics and techniques.

NYT 7/25/43, p3. 950w

WBR 8/1/43, p1. 2300w

———. *Damned to Glory.* New York: Scribner, 1944. 225p

Yarns about the men who fought with P-40s in places like Subic
Bay, Guadalcanal, and Burma are described in cliché-ridden prose
("blasted him to hell," "blew him to bits," "three Japs flamed earth-
ward"), which adulterates the reality of the consummate skill and
courage of American fliers doing battle against the enemy.

NYT 10/22/44, p6. 1000w

WBR 12/24/44, p7. 400w

Scrivener, Jane. *Inside Rome with the Germans*. New York: Macmillan, 1945. 204p

A complete picture by a Catholic of daily life in Rome during the German occupation, covering the time from the Italian armistice in September 1943 to June 1944 when Allied troops entered the city. Given her position, Scrivener speaks with authority that "the nuns here have been magnificent in the midst of bombardments, evacuations, and other tragic circumstances of war. With superhuman strength of mind and body in the teeth of chaos, they have organized, and in the teeth of famine they have fed the hungry and harbored the shelterless."

BW 9/16/45, p11. 650w

NYT 10/7/45, p4. 600w

Seagrave, Gordon. *Burma Surgeon*. New York: Norton, 1943. 295p

Written by an American missionary doctor, only a few chapters of the book deal with the Burma campaign and Seagrave's retreat with General Stilwell from the horrors of war through the jungles to the safety of China.

Nation 8/7/43, 160p. 600w

————. *Burma Surgeon Returns*. New York: Norton, 1946. 268p

Continues the account of a trek from Burma to China and India and the return, with a corps of native nurses, to the ruins and desolation left by the Japanese in Burma. Seagrave also describes the frustration of red tape complicating plans to educate the Burmese people, and considers the part that missions should play.

NYT 5/16/46, p6. 1150w

SRL 5/4/46, p8. 450w

Seaton, George. *Letters to a Soldier*. New York: Dutton, 1943. 93p

An army veteran–father counsels, in guidebook fashion, his son on what to think and how to act while in the service, covering subjects that a newly inducted soldier might need to know: adjustment to military regulations, officers and promotions, friendship and sex, boredom.

Books 9/16/42, p10. 100w

Christian Science Monitor 4/17/42, p18. 340w

Severeid, Eric. *Not So Wild a Dream*. New York: Knopf, 1943. 516p

Brief sketch of Severeid's life, followed by reporting and commentary on the fall of France and the German bombing of London, registering especially hard-hitting chagrin concerning the "criminal" Italian campaign run by bumbling generals wasting many GI lives.

SRL 10/12/46, p23. 1350w

Shackelford, Lynn. *As I See It*. New York: Knopf, 1943. 96p
"Story" drawings of life in the army from rookie days to the end of basic training, by a former member of Disney Hollywood studios.
WBR 12/12/43, p6. 330w

Shacklette, Hansford. *History of the Twelfth Evacuation Hospital*. Nurenberg, 1945. 130p
Details the experiences of hospital personnel from litter bearers and ambulance drivers to nurses and surgeons as they prepared to do their part in the war. The story tells of stateside training and embarkation to England to accompany troops across the battlefields of Europe. Bombing and shelling of the hospital areas were routine. Operations often had to be conducted by flashlight. In reading the accounts of how this organization served, so many things that were an essential part of these operations appear to have been overlooked. These were the ordinary routine jobs, some monotonous and disagreeable, which were regularly and faithfully done. Yet they were as vital to the running of a hospital as the work of the surgeons. Just to say "the hospital operated smoothly here" does not convey the full meaning of the vast quantities of food to be prepared with on-the-clock regularity, the cleaning of dishes and pots, the scrubbing of floors. The reports and other paperwork flowed smoothly, but someone was always pushing a typewriter to make this so. Then there were the guards, standing outside through many uncomfortable hours, giving a sense of security to those who were a part of the activity inside. Transportation never failed to go out because the trips were too long, the roads too muddy, wet, or icy, or the blackout driving too difficult. Included is a roster of the approximately 400 medical personnel who served. Testimonies from various high-ranking officers are part of the appendix. There are two letters from General Patton acknowledging the valuable service performed by the medical staff supporting the troops, boasting "the best medical care" for wounded soldiers. "The promptness and efficiency with which the medical units of the Third Army have performed their duties under extremely difficult conditions of weather, combined with sudden and violent movements, is evinced by the remarkably low death record in this army," Patton wrote.

Shalett, Sidney. *Old Nameless*. New York: Appleton-Century, 1943. 177p
Book offers a vote of confidence for the efficacy of battleships as a weapon of modern war. As commander of a "battlewagon," Shalett describes exploits of his ship and crew during several battles in the South Pacific. The Japanese attacked with squadrons of dive bombers and torpedo planes, and *Old Nameless* responded by knocking

out 32 enemy raiders from the sky and sinking three Japanese battleships. The attitude seeping through this narrative is that every
American sailor is a shining hero and every "Jap" is a detestable vil-
lain.

    BW 7/4/43, p6. 600w

    NYT 6/20/43, p17. 800w

Sharon, Henrietta. *It's Good to Be Alive.* New York: Dodd, 1945.
150p

Work is the result of an effort to boost the morale of soldiers and
sailors, disabled in action, by having a group of artists draw portraits of the wounded men for mailing home to relatives, friends,
and previous employers. Shows hospital routines and patient attitudes, which offered an optimistic glimpse of those on the mend.

    NYT 4/15/45, p24. 340w

Shea, Nancy. *The WAACs.* New York: Harper, 1943. 243p

This is a primer of the world of the Women's Army Auxiliary Corps
(WAACs) describing the induction process, training customs, and
conduct to be observed while in service; includes a glossary of
popular slang.

    NYT 5/30/43, p15. 500w

Sheehan, Vincent. *This House Against This House.* New York: Random House, 1946. 420p

After remarking on the mistakes of the Versailles Treaty and the
hopes of the new United Nations, the straightforward reporting of
Sheehan's personal experiences as an Army staff officer in North
Africa, Italy, India, China, and Germany becomes diffused by opinions. He believes that U.S. politics in North Africa were right, that
U.S. policies in Italy were wrong, and that the problems to be faced
in the postwar world have to be handled by the United Nations and
an "almost daily exercise of reason" in international affairs.

Sherrod, Robert. *Tarawa.* New York: Duell, 1944. 183p

Story of one of the fiercest battles of WWII by a correspondent who
accompanied the troops in landing crafts as they drove toward shore
under heavy enemy fire. Details the chaos of battle by an on-the-
spot reporter, describing spent shells, ripped knapsacks, bomb cra-
ters, emptied gun belts, wrecked ordnance, shattered and fallen
trees, and, most of all, the high cost of gallantry and courage in
American blood and lives fighting to drive Japanese defenders from
a tiny island of sand and coral. In a terse but telling remark, Sherrod
said of the battle for Betio, "What happened only a few days ago on
Tarawa . . . was a dirty, stinking, unromantic battle." Sherrod
wanted to "close the gap between civilian conceptions and the realities of war." He wanted Americans to know not only what war was

really like, but that "we were just beginning to fight the Japs." He seemed determined to expose "wishful thinking, bolstered by comfort-inspiring yarns." The most chilling part of the book is the 32-page roll call at the end, listing 3,500 names of young Marines who had been killed or wounded on the island in only a three-day battle.

    NYT 3/12/44, p1. 1100w

————. *On to Westward: War in the Central Pacific.* New York: Duell, Sloan and Pearce, 1945. 333p

Detailed narrative of war in the Pacific from November 1943 to April 1945, with special focus on the campaigns at Saipan, Iwo Jima, and Okinawa. Like Ernie Pyle, America's most famous war correspondent, Sherrod mentions many American fighters by name and acknowledges the courage, heroism, and sacrifice made by soldiers, sailors, and airmen—reserving his deepest appreciation for the Marines he had come to know, having been so close to them in battle.

    New Yorker 12/1/45, p127. 1050w

    WBR 12/9/45, p4. 1000w

Shiber, Etta; in collaboration with **Anne** and **Paul Dupre**. *Paris Underground.* New York: Scribner, 1943. 390p

A true story by an American woman living in Paris when France fell, providing an inside look into the Paris Underground which, during her involvement, helped over 150 English soldiers escape the Nazis after the evacuation at Dunkirk. When her activities on behalf of the Allied cause were discovered by the Gestapo, Shiber was sent to prison, but she was eventually exchanged for a German spy and returned to America.

    NYT 9/19/43, p1. 1850w

    SRL 9/25/43, p7. 1100w

Shirer, William. *Berlin Diary.* New York: Knopf, 1941. 626p

In this work, made up of notes and parts of broadcasts (before his words were censored), Shirer provides insight into Hitler and the Nazis, on what they had done and what they planned to do, and what the German people thought of it all. Material is supported by quotations from German newspaper headlines and commentaries.

    Books 6/23/41, p1. 1400w

    NYT 6/22/41, p1. 1400w

Singer, K. *Arctic Invasion.* New York, 1944. 30p

Tells of combined American and Norwegian resistance against the German effort to control Iceland and Greenland.

Skattebol, Lars. *The Last Voyage of the Quiem Sabe.* New York: Harper, 1944. 255p

> An unusual personal narrative of Skattebol's experience as a crew member of a cargo ship torpedoed and sunk by a German submarine, forcing him and his shipmates to spend seven dreary days on a raft, suffering from exposure, hunger, thirst, and bitter disappointment at seeing a freighter on the horizon that does not see them, and a growing sense of discouragement amid talk of home, food, girls. During the long ordeal, however—contrary to stories about the enemy's inherent meanness—when the sub surfaced to inspect the wreckage, the Germans gave the survivors directions to help them reach land. Skattebol followed with bitter words against America's neglect for the safety of unescorted merchant ships sailing dangerous waters, finally comparing the climate of racism in the United States to the democratic world on a merchant ship with a crew made up of all nationalities working in harmony together.
>
> *NYT* 8/27/44, p4. 1250w

Skidmore, Hobart. *More Lives Than One.* Boston: Houghton Mifflin, 1943. 265p

> Account by a sergeant in the army of ground personnel—cooks, quartermasters, engineers, dock workers, air service troops, weathermen, mechanics of all trades—the legion of so-called noncombatants whose job it was to support the men in the trenches, yet who sometimes had to fight and die.

Smith, Columbus. *Quentin Reynolds, Officially Dead.* New York: Random House, 1945. 244p

> Account of the experiences of the skipper of the gunboat *Wake*, which was captured by the Japanese, and of his imprisonment and escape with the considerable aid of the Chinese underground and the kind help of many ordinary citizens during his long walk over 700 miles to inland safety.
>
> *WBR* 12/1/45, p3. 1500w

Smith, Douglas M., and **Cecil Carnes**. *American Guerrilla Fighting Behind the Enemy Lines.* Indianapolis, Ind.: Bobbs-Merrill, 1943. 316p

> Offers a running history of guerrilla actions in North Africa and Europe with the purpose of encouraging more support for such groups, and calls on the adoption of guerrilla warfare on a larger scale, using resistance cadres in captive nations to disrupt enemy activities by sabotage and fire fights.
>
> *WBR* 12/12/43, p20. 650w

Smith, Frank. *Battle Diary.* New York: Hobson, 1946.

> Provides a brief outline history of the 243rd Field Artillery Battalion from its activation, through basic training to learn the complex

weapons, followed by a short time spent in England before joining the assault on Normandy beaches. Describes becoming a part of many engagements across Europe, moving heavy guns over rough terrain and often muddy fields, culminating in the Battle of the Bulge and eventually standing fast against the German counter-offensive.

Smith, Nicol, and **Thomas Clark**. *Into Siam*. Indianapolis, Ind.: Bobbs, 1946. 315p

Story of a group of American-educated Siamese carefully trained by the OSS to become spies and to form an underground movement in Thailand (which joined Japan in the war against the United States), reporting on all strategic information the group could gather.

NYT 9/8/46, p31. 500w

WBR 6/9/46, p13. 1000w

Sneed, Bessie. *Captured by the Japanese: Being the Personal Experience of a Miner's Wife Caught in the Philippiness at the Outbreak of World War II*. Denver, Colo.: Bradford-Robinson, 1946. 108p

A sometimes cynical report of a time when "people . . . cease to be human beings and resort to the animal," according to the author, who further explained that it was hard under the strain of war and captivity "to go against the laws of instinct and self-preservation," which after a while meant an "every man for himself" attitude that was adopted by many internees. Counterpoint inferences can be drawn, however, when Sneed tells how nearly 100 people lived to-gether in cramped quarters, on limited rations of food and water, enduring a mostly boring captivity, getting "along . . . well [to-gether] under trying conditions," despite differences in nationalities and ages. In general, the author describes the internment camp as "a melting pot," where "a mother and her children would be assigned sleeping space next to that of a professional prostitute of the China coast; a preacher would be sleeping next to a professional gambler. . . . Sleeping next to me, on one side, was a lovely refined American woman who had traveled widely. . . . Then there was a Russian woman and her daughter, a couple of very refined British women, a woman from Central America, and the prize of the room were two British girls, not so refined . . . together with several others, and with unknown nationality." Inadequate food and water, along with the meanness of some of the guards, was balanced by the dedicated work from army nurses "who had been captured on Corregidor [and] worked hard on no more rations than were issued to the rest of us," treating all sorts of ailments among the 75% of internees who showed signs of pellagra and beri-beri. Whatever the hardships, there were sometimes moments of relief, at the organized concerts, ball games, even an American movie now and then. The worst moments: when starvation led to the killing and eating of stray dogs, even making a meal of "slugs."

Snow, Edgar. *People on Our Side* (Alternate title: *Glory and Bondage*). New York: Random House, 1944. 324p

Along with describing his experiences while visiting countries under the pressure of war—especially China, India, and Russia—Snow offers opinions and judgments on two subjects: the Soviet Union, with analysis of Moscow's probable postwar policies in Eastern Europe, and Asia, and the problem of Asia's future in the wake of the destruction of Tokyo's "prosperity sphere." He believed that the Kremlin did not wish to seek imperialistic expansion into Europe, but desired and intended to set up a series of border states in that region which would, although independent, certainly maintain friendly relations with their giant eastern neighbor.

  NR 10/2/44, p443. 1240w

  NYT 9/10/44, p1. 1750w

Spellman, Francis (Cardinal). *Action This Day*. New York: Scribner, 1943. 250p

A collection of letters to his father in which he tells of the people he met on his visits to the war zones and the religious services he conducted for the fighting men. During extensive travels, he meets and records his impressions of many prominent people: de Gaulle, Franco, Pope Pius XII, Roosevelt, and Churchill.

  Commonweal 1/28/44, p377. 950w

  NYT 12/12/45, p9. 1050w

————. *No Greater Love*. New York: Scribner, 1945. 147p

Spellman's account of the many aspects of war, remarking on the bravery of the fighting men and the unselfish acceptance of sacrifice in the nation's interest, woven into a picture of strong religious feelings among many of the troops. Includes grim stories of suffering on the battlefields and in the hospitals. The soldiers he talked to, in spite of their troubles, were a lot less cynical than some reports would have Spellman believe. The message of the book is that this time the peace that comes must be absolute and lasting.

  Catholic World 11/45, p183. 270w

  Commonweal 8/17/45, p437. 400w

Spencer, Louise. *Guerrilla Wife*. New York: Crowell, 1945. 209p

The wife of an American engineer describes the daily life of a group of miners and missionaries on the run, hiding in the Philippine hills. Helped by sympathetic Filipinos, who warned them of Japanese movements in the area, they received food and clothing and were eventually directed to a submarine that carried them to Australia.

NYT 9/2/45, p4. 750w

Steichen, Edward. *Power in the Pacific*. U.S. Camera (Museum of Modern Art), 1945. 144p

Reproductions of official service photographs of naval combat operation on land, sea, and air that serve to effect a greater understanding of the nature of war in the Pacific.

NYT 6/24/45, p4. 550w

WBR 7/29/45, p4. 220w

Stein, Ralph. *What Am I Laughing At?* New York: McGraw, 1944. 103p

Collection of Sgt. Stein's cartoons, most of which appeared in the army weekly *Yank*. They cover all aspects of army life from the PX to gold brickers and musicians. From sergeants to generals, from censors to cooks, from garbage details to jungle living, from hard salutes to doing camouflage, all of the experiences that reveal the disconnect between a citizen–soldier and the endless variety of occupations in the army.

Steinberg, Saul. *All in Line*. New York: Duell, Sloan & Pearce, 1945. 120p

Satirical sketches by a navy lieutenant of American army life in China, India, North Africa, and Italy. The war pictures of Nazi officers are savage; more engaging portraits of American soldiers characterize their behavior abroad, their tourist disposition in a strange environment, their provincialism contrasted to foreigners.

WBR 6/17/45, p2. 800w

Stern, Michael. *Into the Jaws of Death*. New York: McBride, 1944. 237p

A collection of first-person narratives reporting the experiences of soldiers, sailors, Marines, fliers, and merchant seamen involved in the fighting all over the globe, revealing the "desperate lives [the men] lived, the bitter fight they waged, and the awful fear they felt." Whether from the cockpit of a Flying Fortress as it bumped through a shower of flak, in a PT boat braving a cannon barrage from a Japanese destroyer, or on a foodless raft for weeks drifting aimlessly, "all walked into the Jaws of Death. Some went in with a bitter hatred for the enemy. . . . Some took it as a nasty job that had to be done. Most were unashamedly frightened."

BW 5/14/44, p9. 270w

SRL 6/10/44, p9. 360w

Stevenson, Eleanor, and **Pete Martin**. *I Knew Your Soldier*. New York: Penguin Books, 1944. 237p

This is a story about the Red Cross overseas. It is based on the personal experiences of "Bumpy" Stevenson and her husband, Bill, who was head of the American Red Cross in England and later in North Africa and Italy. Mrs. Stevenson provides a particularly unique woman's slant on the war because she felt it by serving with the soldiers under shell fire on the front lines of battle. Ernie Pyle, the "GI's Correspondent," who knew of Bumpy's kinship with the men, remarked that "she is a sort of roving delegate, cheerer-upper, smoother-over, and finder-outer for the whole Red Cross . . . and half the Army too. She lends her ear to tales of woe, turns her smile on generals and privates without distinction." Stevenson's purpose was to tell the folks back home about the terrible suffering endured by their friends and loved ones, "about the man like the amputation case with the well-worn letter from his fiancee, telling him to forget her if he doesn't come back whole," and a lot of other things besides, both hilariously funny and pathetic.

Stone, Ezra, and **Weldon Melnick**. *Coming Major!* Philadelphia: Lippincott, 1944. 267p

As the creator of the movie character Henry Aldridge, Stone presents a view of the war's "light" side, describing his role as sergeant in the army as keeping up the morale of the men in uniform, directing the Camp Upton Opry House players.

BW 12/3/44, p36. 360w

The Story of the First Armored Division. U.S. Government Printing Office.

Describes many battles and the destruction of countless enemy tanks, guns, and trucks, as well as the capture and supervision of a large number of prisoners (40,000 who surrendered in Africa, 45,000 in Italy).

Stowe, Leland. *No Other Road to Freedom*. New York: Knopf, 1941.

Newspaper dispatches from the Finnish, Norwegian, and Greek fronts represent the core of the book, detailing many months of Stowe's experiences as a war correspondent in these troubled areas. The last five chapters express the opinion that between right and wrong it is irresponsible to remain neutral, and there is a cogent and angry diatribe against American appeasers and isolationists and against complacency in general.

Nation 2/19/44, p224. 900w

WBR 1/16/44, p5. 1450w

―――. *They Shall Not Sleep*. New York: Knopf, 1944. 399p

In a prefatory comment, the author says: "The major portion of the material in this book is based upon the unpublished notes in my war diary from July 1941 to December 1942. In a few chapters, however, I have rewritten incidents and data which were contained in my provocative, opinionated synthesis of the happenings in many

venues (China, Burma, India, Russia) of the war placed in a global
context, with an angry blow against Allied smugness." There are
generally critical portraits of incompetent and corrupt high-ranking
officials, both civilian and military, on the eve of the Japanese invasion of Singapore.

Nation 2/19/44, p224. 900w

WBR 1/16/44, p5. 1450w

————. *Challenge to Freedom.* Greek-American Council, 1945. 30p
The story of what happened in Greece compiled from reports by
Stowe and Constantine Poulas. The tragedy of flaunting the will of
the overwhelming consensus of the Greek people by foreign interests is narrated by Stowe, who explains the civil war in Greece as a
fight between the National Liberation Front—a left-center coalition
of the population's majority—and the Green Mountain Brigade—a
right-wing quasi-fascist group trained and supplied by the British.

Stradling, Harriet. *Johnny.* Salt Lake City: Bookcraft, 1946. 203p
A collection of letters from John S. Stradling, detailing his service
in the army during the war. Most were written to his parents, and a
few to relatives and friends sound the recurring theme that "I have
definite responsibilities to my God, my country, my parents, and
myself." The days he spent in the military preparing for war and going to war made "me realize more and more the real values in life,"
which he described as "righteous living" certain that "my blood will
prove worthy to be shed for my country if necessary." Many of the
letters tell about training for combat in several stateside army
camps, getting used to gunfire and exploding mortar shells, forced
marches, army food and kitchen duty, as well as weekend leaves in
town. It was mostly hard work, but Johnny remained undaunted in
his conviction that "no sacrifice is too great for our nation." Writing
from overseas, he told of his first encounter with "an Arab," and of
the "fun trying to talk to Frenchmen when you don't know . . .
French." His religious faith as a Mormon, however, is the emphasis
in his letters, especially pronounced when he finally became involved in combat in Italy. A Western Union telegram to Johnny's
father dated March 4, 1944, is printed at the end of the book: "We
regret that your son Private First Class John S. Stradling was killed
in action in defense of his country on Seventeen January in Italy."

Taggart, William. *My Fighting Congregation.* Garden City, N.Y.:
Doubleday, 1943. 176p
As told to Christopher Cross, these are reminiscences of an American chaplain who was onboard a troop transport when the news of
the Japanese attack on Pearl Harbor was announced, later remarking
on the number of chaplains who became casualties since war began.

Mirroring the work of chaplains on all battlefronts, Taggart offered the solace of religion for those who wanted it. He found that some men who had not gone to church since childhood sought the comforts of worship in the face of danger, making them better soldiers as well as men.

> *Christian Science Monitor* 1/8/44, p12. 450w
>
> *NYT* 1/23/44, p14. 440w

Target Germany. Anonymous. New York: Simon & Schuster, 1943. 121p

A well-documented narrative recording the early history of the Eighth Air Force bomber command, describing missions flown by the "heavies," which helped end the submarine menace against Allied shipping in the Atlantic. Also describes daily destructive daylight raids on German cities and industries by courageous young men, gripped with tension yet doing an effective job in these hazardous operations.

> *NYT* 12/12/43, p1. 1300w
>
> *WBR* 12/19/43, p1. 1600w

Tartiere, Dorothy, and **Morris Werner**. *The House Near Paris: An American Woman's Story of Traffic in Patriots.* New York: Simon & Schuster, 1946, 317p

Tartiere's efforts to hide downed Allied pilots and aid their escape during four years of German occupation in France—suffering controls, few creature comforts, worry about arousing an informant neighbor's curiosity, the constant fear of discovery, with imprisonment being the nightmare accumulation of life under the Nazis.

> *NYT* 2/24/46, p4. 500w
>
> *WBR* 2/24/46, p2. 1250w

Taylor, Henry. *Time Runs Out.* Garden City, N.Y.: Doubleday, 1942. 333p

Based on observations made while visiting several European nations, the author feared that the war might be lost if the relentless determination of the Nazis was underrated. For Taylor, the most important venue of the conflict was North Africa and the threat to Egypt, arguing that "if Egypt is lost to the Axis, the war is lost."

> *NYT* 5/3/42, p15. 1150w
>
> *SRL* 5/2/42, p11. 750w

———. *Men in Motion.* Garden City, N.Y.: Doubleday, 1943. 306p

Based on trips to Africa and the Near East, this work provides a comprehensive report on the desert war against the Axis, offering a variety of opinions about what Taylor sees as Germany's plan to win the peace even if it loses the war; also about the effects of war upon the future of America. The columnist, James Reston, comments on a number of things he perceives as Taylor's misguided reflections: "Many sincere opponents of the New Deal will question his premise that the Roosevelt Administration is at the root of all our present miseries. . . . And many casual readers of his book will wonder how it could happen that he should be so full of praise for our military accomplishments, so certain that we are the greatest people on earth, so confident in the Christian ideal and yet so dubious about our ability to do business with Stalin and so pessimistic about our prospects of raising the standard of living of any one but ourselves."

SRL 6/5/43, p7. 1600w

WBR 5/30/43, p12. 1500w

———. *Men and Power.* New York: Dodd, 1946. 257p

Based on interviews with prominent world figurers (Franco, Goering, Montgomery, Pope Pius, and others) and his personal and philosophical reactions to all he saw and heard during a whirlwind tour in which he visited many countries around the world—reflections on power and politics within the framework of a German defeat.

NYT 6/23/46, p7. 100w

SRL 7/6/46, p9. 1000w

Tennien, Mark. *Chunking Listening Post.* Creative Age, 1945. 201p

An account by a Roman Catholic priest who spent several years in unoccupied China. Aside from telling how he acted as liaison among hundreds of Maryknoll missionaries while handling their financial affairs, Tennien offers a political assessment favoring Chiang Kai-shek's national government over one supported by the Chinese Communists.

Commonweal 12/14/45, p243. 400w

SRL 12/29/45, p9. 650w

Thomas, Evan. *Ambulance in Africa.* New York: Appleton-Century, 1943. 175p

The son of Norman Thomas—America's foremost socialist—tells of his experiences as a volunteer ambulance driver with the British in Syria and North Africa, reporting on, among other things, the fighting at Tobruck and El Alamein.

WBR 10/24/43, p10. 600w

Thomas, Rowan. *Born in Battle: Round the World Adventures of the 513th Bombardment Squadron.* Philadelphia: Winston, 1944. 367p

Story of how a young lawyer from the South became a fighting air force captain and his many adventures during bombing raids over the Pacific, North Africa, and Italy. The book is based on preserved diaries kept by Thomas and some of his comrades, detailing the many flights and fights of a group known as the "Orphan Squadron."

SRL 7/1/44, p19. 400w

WBR 7/2/44, p19, 250w

Thompson, Lawrance R. *The Navy Hunts the CGR 3070.* Garden City, N.Y.: Doubleday, Doran & Co., 1944. 150p

Stories by crew members about the private yacht *Zaida* that was converted into an auxiliary Coast Guard patrol boat christened *CGR 3070*, whose job it was to reconnoiter for enemy submarines but became "lost" in the Atlantic for three weeks and had to be searched for by the navy. The *Zaida* was one of several sailing vessels in official service manned by "amateur" sailors as sub-watchers.

BW 3/19/44, p8. 360w

NYT 2/6/44, p6. 700w

Thorburn, Lois, and **Donaldson Thorburn**. *No Tumult, No Shouting: The Story of the PRY.* New York: Holt, 1945. 148p

Account of the fight in the Aleutians put up by crews of PBYs when large Japanese forces moved toward taking Alaska; their plans were stymied partly due to the efforts of the gallant airmen who engaged the enemy in Catalinas (hardly made for strenuous combat) and flying in the worst weather imaginable.

BW 6/3/45, p2. 360w

Canadian Forum 6/45, p75. 250w

Thruelsen, Richard, and **Elliott Arnold**. *Mediterranean Sweep: Air Stories from El Alamein to Rome.* New York: Duell, 1944. 278p

More than 50 true stories of the human side of aerial warfare have been collected in this book at the encouragement of Lieut. Gen. Ira C. Eaker, commanding general of the Mediterranean Allied Air Forces. They range from mere wisps of anecdotes to detailed, illuminating accounts of some of the major episodes of that long campaign. Not devoted exclusively to the deeds of American or British fliers, there are tales of French pilots, like those who relentlessly bombed the airfields at Tunis even at the risk of killing their own families in nearby houses; of South Africans, Australians, Yugoslavs, and Greeks. One of the best tells the adventures of the American flight nurses who were forced down in Yugoslavia and spent months with the Partisans before they were rescued.

NYT 11/19/44, p6. 300w

Tobin, Richard. *Invasion Journal.* New York: Dutton, 1944. 223p

A narrative filled with subjective speculations of events leading up to the D-Day invasion at Normandy, in which the author expresses uneasy concern about the robot flying bombs that the Nazis sent over London, pointing to their growing significance as weapons of war, yet criticizing Churchill's social planning for peace being fraught with a Middle Ages mentality.

NYT 10/8/44, p10. 550w

SRL 10/14/44, p50. 700w

Tower, Hansel. *Fighting the Devil with the Marines.* Dorrance, 1945. 172p

A narrative by a navy chaplain of his experiences and observations from three years stationed among Marines on the battlefields of the South Pacific, with concluding remarks connecting the impact of the war to the manners and morals of the men who fought it.

Springfield Republican 9/14/45, p6. 340p

Treaner, Thomas. *One Damn Thing after Another: The Adventures of an Innocent Man Trapped between Public Relations and the Axis.* Garden City, N.Y.: Doubleday, 1944. 294p

Light-hearted account of the several months Treaner spent as a correspondent covering the war in many places: among the troops at the Anzio beachhead, crossing the Rapido River with advancing GIs in the Italian campaign, riding with crews through flak-filled skies during an air raid over Rome, battling the brass about how to handle stories of a successful battle—all told with a truly personal touch that gives a feel more about the man himself than the war he covered.

NYT 8/6/44, p4. 600w

SRL 8/12/33, p25. 700w

Treat, Ida. *The Anchored Heart.* New York: Harcourt, 1941. 314p

An American woman married to a French sea captain reveals the strengths and weaknesses of the French character through her observations of what Bretons, on the German-occupied island off the coast of Brittany, thought about the war and what effect the occupation had on their lives.

Books 10/16/41, p5. 950w

Christian Science Monitor 12/27/41, p10. 650w

Tregaskis, Richard. *Guadalcanal Diary.* New York: Random House, 1943. 263p

In a series of diary entries, Tregaskis reports on the offshore naval bombardment against the Japanese defenders of Guadalcanal, the beachhead landings, and the arduous jungle fighting assigned to the Marine invasion force. While action is described, it is generally brief; the tough fighting, great destruction, and casualties scarcely dwelled on. In fact, Tregaskis reports little heavy, close-up fighting, with only oblique references to casualties, often just of the wounded who survived. The book indulges the somewhat sunny conceit of men sent ashore on a hostile enemy-held island, fraught with danger and possible serious injury and death, far away from home and loved ones, yet undaunted.

————. *Invasion Diary.* New York: Random House, 1944. 245p

A day-by-day record catalogs the weary, cautious, brave, frightened, determined soldiering done by those who won hard-fought victories in Sicily and the Italian mainland against a tenacious German army. Because Tregaskis himself suffered a serious head wound, some of the best parts of the book deal with the physical and psychological reactions of the many GIs wounded in battle. Beyond the personal, Tregaskis reports on the American policy of allowing "the Italians to run their own country" when peace is restored, even if it meant filling government agencies with "many competent officials who have been active Fascists—men who wore a party button only because they couldn't get a job otherwise. We don't want to remove a man because he had been practically forced to become a Fascist, if he is a competent man."

> *BW* 8/20/44, p1. 1200w
> *NYT* 8/20/44, p7. 700w

Trumbull, Robert. *The Raft.* New York: Holt, 1942. 205p

A narrative by the chief editor of the *Honolulu Advertiser*, from a story told him by Chief Machinist Mate Dixon, of three navy airmen flying a reconnaissance mission in search of Japanese submarine activity when they ran out of gas and had to ditch in the sea. For 34 days across more than 1,000 miles of open ocean, the downed fliers struggled to stay afloat on a 4'x8' rubber raft that "turned them like birds on a spit beneath [a flaming sun] every day." Inevitably, the heat, cold, hunger, tedium, and strain affected their minds, and all had manifestations of delirium. They thought about dying and an afterlife, even discussed cannibalism. Yet, they stubbornly fought off despair and defeat by prayer and thoughts of home and by eating fish and drinking rainwater.

> *Books* 8/23/42, p1. 1750w
> *NYT* 8/23/42, p3. 1200w

————. *Silversides.* New York: Holt, 1945. 270p

Describes the personalities, duties, and responsibilities of each officer and man aboard the submarine *Silversides* during a search-and-destroy mission in the Pacific, which accounted for nearly 100 tons of enemy shipping damaged or sunk.

> *BW* 8/23/45, p1. 1150w
> *NYT* 8/19/45, p5. 1050w

Tweed, George. *Robinson Crusoe, USN*. New York: McGraw, 1945. 267p

Describes the adventures of a navy man stranded on Guam after the Japanese takeover, living for more than two years in caves and makeshift shelters, all the while hunted by enemy soldiers and helped by natives with food and clothing until his rescue in the summer of 1944.

   NYT 4/15/45, p6. 950w
   WBR 4/8/45, p4. 950w

Vail, Margaret. *Yours Is the Earth*. Philadelphia: Lippincott, 1944. 287p

An American wife of a French diplomat describes the daily process of living in occupied France, both in the country and in Paris, acknowledging how much comfort and modest freedom of movement a woman of means could still enjoy. Filled with sketches of dispirited ordinary citizens and local color of places she traveled to in her flight to Spain, Portugal, and, finally, to America.

   BW 4/30/44, p8. 500w
   WBR 4/30/44, p2. 1000w

Valtin, Jan. *Children of Yesterday*. Reader's Press, 1946. 429p

As a combat correspondent with the Twenty-Fourth Infantry, Valtin tells how his outfit helped liberate the Philippines, providing an insider's view of war with all its savagery and blood—showing the lows to which ordinary humans (yesterday's children) in an extraordinary human activity can sink, such as becoming "souvenir hunters," fieldstripping "the Nips, [kicking] the gold teeth out of their mouths . . . something the folks back home didn't read about."

   WBR 8/25/46, p10. 500w

Vetter, Ernest. *Death Was Our Escort*. New York: Prentice-Hall, 1944. 323p

Chapters such as "The Art of Sniping" and "Hide and Seek with the Japs" tell of the dangers that American PT boat crews faced when doing battle against heavy odds with enemy submarines, cruisers, and transports in the waters around New Guinea.

   WBR 12/10/44, p2. 800w

Wade, Harry. *Five Miles Closer to Heaven: An Adventure by Parachute over the Jungles of India*. Ligurian Pamphlet Office, 1945. 60p

Tells of the successful and sometimes unsuccessful adventures flying over the "Hump" by young Americans—from every walk of life and background—ready to give their lives to keep open the lifelines of supplies from India to China.

Wagg, Harry. *A Million Dead.* Nicholas and Watson, 1943. 192p

The knowledge that seven million died in China, with fifty million more made homeless, convinced Wagg that the policies of western nations in dealing with peoples of the Far East had been futile and needed changing. Wagg believed that the co-prosperity notion advanced for the area by Japan seemed a fair-enough concept, even prior to the outbreak of war.

Wainwright, Jonathan. *General Wainwright's Story.* Garden City, N.Y.: Doubleday, 1941. 314p

Large portions of the book deal with the hopeless retreat and ultimate surrender on Bataan and Corregidor to superior forces; the rest tells the story of Wainwright's long captivity and of Japanese brutality toward their war prisoners.

　　NYT 4/7/46, p7. 1250w

　　WBR 4/7/46, p3. 1650w

Walters, Maude, ed. *Combat in the Air.* New York: Appleton-Century, 1945. 275p

A miscellany of firsthand experiences by airmen, with their stories told for them by a variety of newsmen (W. L. White, Quentin Reynolds, A. J. Liebling, Eric Severeid, for instance—all of whom wrote their own personal narratives). Representative titles: "Bombers to Britain," "Over the Hump," "Target: Ploesti," "Death in the Dark," "My Air Duel with Mussolini."

　　BW 12/17/45, p5. 90w

Warde, Beatrice. *Bombed but Unbroken.* Typophiles Books, 1941. 100p

A limited-edition (500 copies) collection of commentaries from a diary kept by Warde of her life in London during the German air raids. Warde achieved the merit of a mutual consciousness with the essence of the British experience in the war, publicly working for the common cause and privately tending to small domestic matters.

　　NYT 7/13/41, p17. 270w

Warfield, Hania, and **Gaither Warfield.** *Call Us to Witness.* Aurora, Calif.: Ziff-Davis 1945. 434p

Two American missionaries stranded in Poland at the outbreak of war until the winter of 1942 tell their story—absent of history, politics, and propaganda—of what they endured during the German occupation. As members of the Methodist Church in Warsaw, they did what they could to aid friends being hounded by the Nazis.

　　BW 7/15/45, p3. 550w

　　WBR 7/15/45, p5. 900w

We the Forty-Eighth. Heidelberg: Brausdruck, 1945. 352p

This is the full story of the wartime experiences of the 600 officers and men of an Engineer Combat Battalion, each with different personalities and different ways of thinking, boasting of the American soldier's gift for self-initiative and imagination, along with a high order of intelligence and ability. The "route" traced in this history of the "Forty-Eighth" began—after stateside training—with an ocean voyage to Africa, then to Italy, followed by a landing in southern France, ultimately to fight its way into Germany. The story tells of these "pick and shovel" soldiers who rode "recon" with a squad truck, lived in holes cuddled up with an M-1, served as temporary MPs, quartermasters, ordnance, cavalry, and infantry riflemen. All the while, they built bridges across several rivers in Italy, France, and Germany and cleared the way to Cassino and other places that were left obstacle-ridden by the retreating enemy.

Weller, George. *Singapore Is Silent.* New York: Harcourt, 1943. 312p.

An eyewitness account by a war correspondent of the fall of Singapore, including cogent details of the fighting and the retreat down the Malay Peninsula, what actions were taken to stall the enemy's advance and to what effect. For the most part, according to Weller, it was a "boy at the dike" sort of resistance, only waiting for the United States to assume the major burden of the war in the Pacific. He held the firm belief that Japan was "not merely America's enemy for this war alone, as perhaps are Germany and Italy; it is America's enemy for all time."

Wells, Charles. *A Veteran Came Home Today.* Friendship Press, 1945. 23p

Describes the feeling of relief for men who no longer had to be separated from loved ones by oceans, mountains, jungles, and the duties of war. Wells preaches the positive lesson that Americans learned from their trying wartime experiences. "He may be a Negro, or an Oriental, or his ancestors may have been Viking or Pilgrim Father, Slavs, or Jews. Whoever he is, he knows now that racial equality is no longer a theory to men who have fought together, saved each other's lives, and shared cigarettes without regard to race or creed."

Wertenbaker, Charles, and Robert Capa. *Invasion!* New York: Appleton-Century, 1944. 168p

Writer and cameraman tell the story of the D-Day invasion and of the men, high and low, who took part in it, with illuminating text and photographs covering the beachhead days, the occupation of Cherbourg, and the entrance into Paris. Also included are admiring

biographies of General Omar Bradley and General Bedell Smith and
a not-so-flattering pass at General George Patton.

> *BW* 9/3/44, p1. 1150w
>
> *SRL* 10/7/44, p15. 850w

West, Levon (pseud. Ivan Dmitri). *Flight to Everywhere*. New York:
McGraw, 1944. 240p

This is the pictorial record of Ivan Dmitri's flights with the United
States Army Air Transport Command from New York to China by
way of Africa, and from China back to New York by way of Iceland. There are 150 photographs in color and some 300 more in
black and white. Accompanying the pictures is Dmitri's story of his
flights—part travelogue, but in the main an account of the incredible accomplishments of the Army Transport Command.

Westrate, Edwin. *Forward Observer*. New York: Dutton, 1944. 179p

A personal narrative that reads more like a novel. It includes a puer-
ile love affair with a Hollywood-type Wac, which distracts from the
factual depictions of how artillery units go about their business in
determining their targets through the use of forward observer teams
of telephone linemen and radio operators. Some believe that gathering and relaying intelligence about enemy positions is the "most
dangerous job in the army."

> *BW* 3/19/44, p11. 340w
>
> *NYT* 4/2/44, p12. 500w

Wettlin, Margaret. *The Russian Road*. Progress Books, 1945. 126p

Experiences of an American woman in Russia from the first day of
the German invasion and for the next three years.

Wheeler, Keith. *The Pacific Is My Beat*. New York: Dutton, 1943.
383p

This is a record of what Wheeler saw, heard, and felt in the first
year after Pearl Harbor was attacked by the Japanese. Many months
were spent aboard ships of the Pacific fleet, with army and navy fliers in the Aleutians, with the troops that seized and held a strip of
Aleutian tundra, and where they fought to prevent the Japanese
from taking control of any more islands in the chain.

> *NYT* 11/14/43, p3. 650w
>
> *WBR* 11/14/43, p5. 1650w

———. *We Are the Wounded*. New York: Dutton, 1945. 224p

Wheeler's reflections during his convalescence in a Hawaiian hospital after sustaining serious wounds during the bitter fight for Iwo
Jima, remarking how the injured were treated on the battlefield, in
rear medical stations, and at fully equipped and staffed hospitals.

> *SRL* 12/15/45, p28. 650w
>
> *WBR* 12/16/45, p4. 700w

White, Leigh. *Long Balkan Nights*. New York: Scribner, 1944. 473p

Within the context of White's "admitted" prejudices—opposition to totalitarianism, favoring democracy—the book outlines the problems in the wartime Balkans and the political difficulties which lay ahead in that corner of the world. White was filled with outrage about the divisive politics practiced by the Slovenes and Croats, playing into the hands of the invading Germans, handicapping the valiant and admirable efforts of the Serbs in resisting the Nazis.

NYT 2/27/44, p4. 1000w

WBR 3/5/44, p4. 900w

White, Margaret, Bourke- *Shooting the Russian War*. New York: Simon & Schuster, 1942. 298p

With accompanying text, this is essentially a visual documentary consisting of more than 100 photographs from a personal and reportorial perspective, showing the effects of German air raids on Moscow as well as portraits of Stalin and candid shots of what the war was like to ordinary Russians.

NYT 7/19/42, p3. 650w

SRL 8/22/42, p10. 600w

————. *They Called It "Purple Heart Valley."* New York: Simon & Schuster, 1944. 202p

Sixteen pages of battlefield photographs integrated with more than 150 pages of text, authentically recording the voices of the fighting men, which gave some meaning to what White called "the ordered insanity of war." Also highlighted is the exceptional bravery exhibited by American nurses tending the wounded close to the battle line.

NYT 11/26/44, p7. 900w

WBR 12/10/44, p1. 100w

White, Walter. *Rising Wind*. Garden City, N.Y.: Doubleday, 1945. 155p

A disturbing report by the executive secretary of the NAACP on racial bigotry as an official policy of the U.S. military, although White points to the fact that race relations are better abroad than at home, and concludes that in the exigencies of war the lessons learned when black and white soldiers work and fight together may have a beneficial influence in establishing respect and tolerance for African Americans in postwar America.

White, William. *Journey for Margaret* New York: Harcourt, 1941. 256p

Part of the book is a record of his witness to London victimized by German bombs, as with the Christopher Wren church consumed in flames. Another part is the record of how he and his wife searched for and ultimately found an orphaned English girl to adopt, showing the contrast between the inhuman torment of war and a reflective human gesture of caring.

   NYT 12/21/41, p9. 600w

   Springfield Republican 12/16/41, p7. 650w

———. *They Were Expendable.* New York: Harcourt, 1942. 209p

The story of the part played by MTB Squadron Three in the Philippine campaign, as told to the author by four of its young officers: Bulkeley, Kelly, Akers, and Cox. These men were responsible for transporting General MacArthur safely to Australia. This and their many other exploits, from the time when the first Japanese planes came over Manila Bay until the destruction of their brave little flotilla, have as background "the whole tragic panorama of the Philippine campaign—America's little Dunkirk." The title White chose for the book signaled the theme that in war, high-ranking officials sometimes consider men (and everything else for that matter) more easily and efficiently replaced than rescued or protected. White admitted to not fully comprehending the young naval officer who said, "We were expendable. . . . They are expending you and that machine gun to get time. They don't expect to see either one again." It troubled him to think that American military leaders knowingly sacrificed lives to stall the Japanese perhaps a minute or two, and that sailors were ordered to hold positions until killed or captured. "You see," explained Lt. Bulkeley, "we were expendable. . . . It's like this: In a war, anything can be [considered] expendable—money, gasoline, equipment, or men. . . . You know the situation and you don't mind."

   NYT 9/13/42, p1. 1250w

   SRL 9/12/42, p5. 1000w

———. *Queens Die Proudly.* New York: Harcourt, 1943. 273p.

Story of a Flying Fortress emblazoned on the side of its nose with a Disney cartoon-image of a hybrid bird—half swan and half goose—dubbed "The Swoose." Underneath the Swoose, there appeared the unpretentious statement, "It Flies," playing off the plane's ragged appearance and marginal functionality. The Swoose muddled through a series of actions across a wide landscape from the Philippines to Borneo and Java to Australia. Ultimately, the plane was demoted to transport missions because of its unworthy fighting fitness. *Queens Die Proudly* chronicles the odyssey of a fighter bomber and its crew, from a narrow survival during the Japanese raid near Manila, through months of dangerous engagements. Though the machine was overmatched, it helped disrupt the enemy's advance in all sectors until it was relieved of duty. Vivid descriptions of heroism, gallantry, and saving humor of a crew faced with danger, fatigue, pain, and a tragic scarcity of equipment.

>   *NYT* 6/6/43, p1. 1200w
>   *SRL* 6/5/43, p9. 1650w

————. *Report on the Russians.* New York: Harcourt, 1945. 309p

A mix of complimentary and mostly uncomplimentary views of the Russians and their country under the Soviet system. Deprecating the drab primitiveness of Soviet life, White rails against a society whose freedom is captive to dictatorship authority and unlimited bureaucracy.

>   *BW* 3/25/45, p5. 950w
>   *Canadian Forum* 5/45, p46. 1200w

Whittaker, James. *We Thought We Heard the Angels Sing.* New York: Dutton, 1943. 139p

A third account of 21 days adrift with seven companions on three inflated rafts in the vast Pacific, emphasizing the part played by faith for survival. In Whittaker's book, the rough waves of suffering and a bleak despair that became almost palpable took on religious rather than physical overtones. For him—different from Rickenbacker (*Seven Came Through*) and even Bartek (*Life Out There*)—the drifting experience was more of the spiritual odyssey of one who began as an indifferent sort of agnostic and ended as a confirmed believer in a Supreme Being and the mysterious ways in which God visited trials on men in order to test their faith in this world as a prelude to saving them for the next.

>   *NYT* 3/28/43, p7. 750w
>   *WBR* 3/21/43, p1. 700w

Wilcox, Richard. *Of Men and Battle.* San Francisco: Howell, 1944. 124p

Pen-and-ink and wash drawings with captions and comments depicing the anger and fear in the faces of those who stormed the enemyheld beach on Arawa, New Britain, which was to be taken and held at any cost.

>   *WBR* 10/15/44. 450w

Wilkie, Wendell. *One World.* New York: Simon & Schuster, 1943. 206p

Wilkie's basic thought has to do with recognition of a planet that is growing smaller and smaller, making all people and nations ever nearer to each other and ever more interdependent. The book is a plea for understanding and cooperation among peoples everywhere, and an appeal for democratic self-governments and the creation of international machinery to keep the peace, with justice and freedom for all.

Ethics 10/43, p5. 2000w

Political Science Quarterly 9/43, p426. 1450w

Willard, Warren. *The Leathernecks Come Through*. Grand Rapids, Mich.: Revel, 1944. 224p

Describes the dual job a chaplain performs with the Marines engaged in battles, tending to the physical needs of the wounded, saving their bodies, and saving their souls through prayer. During six months of fighting in the Solomons, he was hoping to inspire a bit of peace and gentleness of spirit in an attempt to counter the pain and dread and hate that overwhelms men in war.

NYT 12/10/44, p20. 280w

Willis, George. *Surreptitious Entry*. New York: Appleton-Century, 1946. 214p

During the war, Willis was an undercover agent in Naval Intelligence. The spy-tracking stories he tells are supposed to be true.

San Francisco Chronicle 11/19/46, p14. 550w

Willoughby, Amea. *I Was on Corregidor*. New York: Harper, 1943. 249p

Experiences of an American official's wife in the war-torn Philippines, enduring weeks of Japanese bombing at Corregidor before she was taken by submarine to safety in Australia. The author talks about the alternating moods of hope and despair connected to reports of help on the way and disappointment when it did not arrive, and the strains put on Filipino loyalty under the seductive appeal of the Japanese propaganda barrage proclaiming the Far East Brotherhood.

NYT 6/6/43, p6. 600w

WBR 6/20/43, p6. 800w

Wilson, Earl, et al. *Betio Beachhead*. New York: Putnam, 1945.

Promoted as being the United States Marines' own story of the assault on the Tarawa atoll, it was documented and written by Marine combat correspondents who went through the battle. The same, yet different, as Robert Sherrod's personal narrative *Tarawa*, *Betio Beachhead* takes on the classic character of a textbook rendering, in which each Marine was not more than any piece of equipment they brought to battle.

Wilson, Ruth (Danenhower). *Jim Crow Joins Up*. Garden City, N.Y.: Doubleday, 1945. 182p

A white woman reports the findings of a study on the status of African Americans in the armed forces, made from visits to 22 military posts and stations throughout the United States. Wilson's findings were reviewed by the public relations offices of both the army and navy and "amended" by them before the report was published. The author describes the things that individual officers, soldiers, civilians, and government departments did to individual Negro soldiers. Some good; far more downright evil. Wilson provides a particularly valuable report on the status of black women in the services, and has hopeful things to say about the integrated training in the Officer Candidate Schools and the generous racial attitudes in the Marines. "But there are few places in the Army or Navy where all men are treated as men, all women as women, and all as patriotic American citizens."

    SRL 3/3/45, p10. 650w

Winston, Robert. *Aces Wild*. Garden City, N.Y.: Holiday, 1942. 320p
Story of an American test pilot in Europe during the middle of 1940 who taught Finnish aviators to fly.

    Books 1/1/42, p3. 480w

————. *Fighting Squadron*. Garden City, N.Y.: Holiday, 1946. 182p
A veteran squadron leader's firsthand account of carrier combat with Task Force 58, most of the action taking place in and around the Marshalls and the Philippines. In telling the history of his "Meataxe Squadron," Commander Winston underscores the types of preparation and routine required on a wartime carrier.

    Library Journal 10/15/46, p1468. 100w

Wise, James. *Very Truly Yours*. New York: Dial Press, 1943. 208p
A collection of letters from Americans in all branches of the service, at home and overseas, which, according to the editor, "come from all parts of the nation, and from men and women of different creeds and races, and in every walk of life," from former lumberjacks to taxi drivers, from tough army regulars to softer bemused conscripts ranging from the semiliterate to the educated.

    BW 11/14/42, p18. 450w

Wolfert, Ira. *The Battle for the Solomons*. Boston: Houghton, 1943. 200p
An eyewitness account of the fighting in and around the Solomons that was supposed to serve two purposes. 1) To assuage the worries and doubts of the folks back home, citing statistics calculated to make the readers feel confident that "about four hundred Jap planes have been destroyed by us, on the ground, in the air. . . . In the same period, the Japs have shot down two of our Flying Fortresses." 2) To explain in layman's terms that the war was being fought in that remote sector of the world "for islands to be used primarily as unsinkable aircraft carriers."

    Nation 2/20/43, p277. 700w
    NYT 1/17/43, p3. 1500w

————. *Torpedo 8*. Boston: Houghton, 1943. 127p

By the author of *The Battle for the Solomons*, *Torpedo 8* is the story of an American bomber squadron that—after the Battle of Midway in which five of its six planes were lost—took for its motto: "Attack and Vengeance." Describing the air battles as maneuvering among swarms of other planes with Americans and Japanese attacking and being attacked, Wolfert describes the experience as almost a fantasy, made more so by the grim and deadly work at hand that removes it all from reality.

————. *American Guerrilla in the Philippines*. New York: Simon & Schuster, 1945. 301p

A true story of Lt. I. D. Richardson who was shipwrecked on Japanese-occupied Leyte where he joined with a guerrilla band engaged in acts of sabotage against the Japanese garrison and communicated information about enemy movements on one of the islands in the Philippine archipelago. Contributing to these efforts, Richardson helped to create telegraph lines from barbed wire, bullets from brass curtain rods, and fuel from distilled alcohol, all the while carrying on a love affair with a Filipino woman.

   NR 5/21/45, p713. 1250w
   NYT 4/22/45, p1. 2000w

Wordell, Malcolm, and **Edwin Seiler**. *Wildcats over Casablanca*. Boston: Little, 1943. 309p

Tells of a squadron of Gruman Wildcats, based on an offshore carrier, taking part in covering the first American military landings on North African shores—a mission in which Lt. Wordell was shot down and taken prisoner. The latter part of the book focuses on the political quandary faced by the Free French during the impending American occupation of their territory.

   NYT 6/13/43, p4. 750w
   SRL 7/3/43, p16. 750w

Wynn, E. J. *Bombers Across*. New York: Dutton, 1944. 178p

Author's story from his barnstorming flying days in the 1930s to when he became a "Yank in the Royal Canadian Air Force" and was given the job of ferrying men and planes across the ocean to lands where they were needed, admitting to long hours of boredom and moments of worry and fear through many dangerous flights.

   NYT 7/30/44, p20. 440w
   WBR 9/20/44, p2. 500w

***Yank*, the Army Weeky**. New York: Dutton, 1945. 304p

A collection of stories, poems, cartoons, and personal comments, which go a long way toward conveying the war from an enlisted man's point of view, while showing how the American soldier does his job without joy but faithfully and well in the "deadly, bloody, and filthy" business of war.

NYT 4/22/45, p3. 900w

WBR 4/22/45, p1. 1500w

Yoder, Robert. *There's No Front Like Home.* Boston: Houghton, 1944. 115p

Mild-mannered, cracker-barrel satires about the hard life endured by civilians on the home front, facing taxes, gas rationing, servant shortages, and the perilous adventure of raising a victory garden, indicated by such typical articles as "Texas Will Beat the Axis," "Out of Gas," and "Should a Lady Thumb?"

NYT 4/2/44, p8. 120w

WBR 5/14/44, p14. 170w

Zanuck, Darryl. *Tunis Expedition.* New York: Random House, 1943. 160p

Zanuck, the movie studio head, writes: "D-Day! This Is It! The battle for North Africa has begun! News flashes into the War Room from every point of contact. A sea battle rages off Casablanca! Our troops are landing at Algiers and Oran! The French are resisting!" During December-November fighting, Zanuck supervised a contingent of cameramen to produce footage of American military activity in and around the vast territories along the Mediterranean coast. The primary objects of this task were: 1) convey information to the war department, 2) provide news pictures for release to the public, 3) provide historical pictorial records of the war.

NYT 4/11/43, p15. 800w

WBR 4/11/43, p3. 700w

ABOUT THE AUTHORS

Hildy Neel presently teaches at Rochester Community and Technical College in Rochester, Minnesota. Previously she has taught courses in American and English literature at Northwestern University in Evanston, Illinois; St. Thomas University in St. Paul, Minnesota; Long Island University in Brookville, New York; and the College of William and Mary in Williamsburg, Virginia, where she earned a Ph.D. in American Studies. This annotated bibliography grew out of her doctoral dissertation focusing on the history of World War II personal narratives. Dr. Neel's other publications include a number of articles, several involving Hemingway and Fitzgerald. Currently she is working on a fabulist element in the short stories of Hemingway.

Arthur Coleman has been a college professor for nearly fifty years, twenty of which he served as chairman of the English Department at C.W. Post campus of Long Island University. More than twenty of his articles on various aspects of American literature have been published in literary and scholarly journals. His resume includes four book-length bibliographies—two on English and American drama and two on epic and metrical romances. He has also written two novels.